Late Antiquity: A Very Short Introduction

D1445781

VERY SHORT INTRODUCTIONS are for anyone wanting a stimulating and accessible way in to a new subject. They are written by experts, and have been published in more than 25 languages worldwide.

The series began in 1995, and now represents a wide variety of topics in history, philosophy, religion, science, and the humanities. The VSI Library now contains over 200 volumes—a Very Short Introduction to everything from ancient Egypt and Indian philosophy to conceptual art and cosmology—and will continue to grow to a library of around 300 titles.

Very Short Introductions available now:

Available soon:

For more information visit our web site
www.oup.com/vsi/

Gillian Clark

LATE ANTIQUITY

A Very Short Introduction

OXFORD
UNIVERSITY PRESS

OXFORD
UNIVERSITY PRESS

Great Clarendon Street, Oxford ox2 6DP

Oxford University Press is a department of the University of Oxford.
It furthers the University's objective of excellence in research, scholarship,
and education by publishing worldwide in

Oxford New York

Auckland Cape Town Dar es Salaam Hong Kong Karachi
Kuala Lumpur Madrid Melbourne Mexico City Nairobi
New Delhi Shanghai Taipei Toronto

With offices in

Argentina Austria Brazil Chile Czech Republic France Greece
Guatemala Hungary Italy Japan Poland Portugal Singapore
South Korea Switzerland Thailand Turkey Ukraine Vietnam

Oxford is a registered trade mark of Oxford University Press
in the UK and in certain other countries

Published in the United States
by Oxford University Press Inc., New York

© Gillian Clark 2011

The moral rights of the author have been asserted
Database right Oxford University Press (maker)

First published 2011

All rights reserved. No part of this publication may be reproduced,
stored in a retrieval system, or transmitted, in any form or by any means,
without the prior permission in writing of Oxford University Press,
or as expressly permitted by law, or under terms agreed with the appropriate
reprographics rights organization. Enquiries concerning reproduction
outside the scope of the above should be sent to the Rights Department,
Oxford University Press, at the address above

You must not circulate this book in any other binding or cover
and you must impose the same condition on any acquirer

British Library Cataloguing in Publication Data

Data available

Library of Congress Cataloging in Publication Data

Data available

Typeset by SPI Publisher Services, Pondicherry, India
Printed in Great Britain by
Ashford Colour Press Ltd, Gosport, Hampshire

ISBN 978-0-19-954620-6

3 5 7 9 10 8 6 4 2

Contents

Acknowledgements

To friends and colleagues in the Society for Late Antiquity, the Oxford Centre for Late Antiquity, and the South West and Wales Regional Network; to authors and co-editors of *TTH* and OECS; and to the OUP readers, all of whom showed how much more there is to learn and how different this *Very Short Introduction* could be.

List of illustrations

Late Antiquity

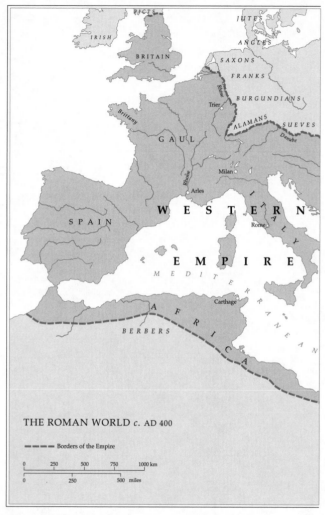

Map: The Roman world in late antiquity

THE ROMAN WORLD *c.* AD 400

- - - - Borders of the Empire

| 0 | 250 | 500 | 750 | 1000 km |

| 0 | 250 | 500 miles |

VANDALS

HUNS

GOTHS

○ Sirmium

Balkans

Danube

Constantinople ○

Hadrianopolis ✕

GOTHS

Caucasus Mnts

E A S T E R N

Greece

Asia Minor

Tigris

PERSIA

○ Ephesus

○ Antioch

Euphrates

E M P I R E

S Y R I A

Levant

S E A

Alexandria ○

EGYPT

Nile

Chapter 1
What and when is late antiquity?

Late antiquity saw the fall of Rome and the survival of Rome. It saw medieval Europe formed from post-Roman 'barbarian' kingdoms, and Byzantium adapting to dramatic loss of territory and to new opponents and allies. It saw the impact of two new religious movements, Christianity and Islam, on the world ruled by Rome. Roman law and Jewish Talmud were codified, Christian creeds were formulated and the canon of Judaeo-Christian scripture was established, and the Qur'an was composed. New generations worked with the ancient traditions of classical literature and philosophy, art and architecture. Christian copyists, and translators into Syriac and Arabic, helped to transmit these resources to the Middle Ages and the Renaissance.

Fifty years ago, 'late antiquity' was rarely used as a name for the period of transition which began in the early 4th century with Constantine, the first Christian emperor, and which ended with the ending of Roman imperial rule, in the late 5th century for the West and the late 7th century for the Near East. This period was known to classicists as 'late Roman', to Byzantinists as 'early Byzantine', and to medievalists as 'early medieval'. In those fifty years, research has extended the boundaries of late antiquity in time and space, taking in (at least) the 3rd and 8th centuries, challenging the Roman perspective on non-Roman cultures, and refusing to accept the grand narratives of Christian triumph over paganism and Dark Age decline from the glories of Roman empire. Many academic disciplines meet here: classics and medieval studies, history and archaeology, linguistics and literature, theology and visual arts. All reflect on what they do and why, and all keep in touch in the age of the Internet.

So what is late antiquity? If it is always 'early' or 'late' something else, what makes it a distinct phase of human history? It is easier to see a contrast than to define a frontier. To begin with an example:

> These Romans are hostile to the name of Christ, even though for Christ's sake the barbarians spared them. In the sack of the city, the shrines of the martyrs and the churches of the apostles gave refuge to their own and to outsiders.

The city of Rome in the early 5th century is seen here through the words of Augustine, bishop of Hippo, in his great work *City of God*. It looks dramatically different from classical Rome four centuries before. In AD 410, Gothic barbarians sacked the city: this had not happened for 800 years, since the Gauls invaded in 390 BC. (Provided, said Augustine, you disregard all the times when Romans invaded Rome in civil war.) The Goths showed respect for Christian churches and for shrines commemorating Christian martyrs, who had been executed on the orders of Roman officials. For three centuries after the crucifixion of Jesus Christ, his followers were at risk of death by torture if they refused to worship the gods of Rome. But in Rome of 410, the temples of Rome's gods survived as architectural heritage, their sacrifices and rituals banned by the laws of Christian emperors.

Some refugees from the Goths claimed that 'Christian times' made it possible for barbarians to sack the city, because the gods who protected Eternal Rome were angry at Christian neglect. This claim was challenged by Augustine, bishop of a small town on the North African coast. Before he became a bishop, Augustine used his own ability, and the resources of family, patrons, and networks, to move from an even smaller North African town. He taught rhetoric, the art of public speaking, first in the regional capital Carthage, then in Rome, then in Milan, which was one of the residences of the imperial court. He gave up his career, and the prospect of marriage, for what he saw as the true Christian life of prayer and Bible study, and he led this life first in a household community, then as a priest and bishop who taught his people and gave them pastoral care. He catalogued his many writings, and they survived to make him one of the most influential presences in Western culture.

Here is the world of late antiquity. New ethnic groups merge, or conflict, with the population of the Roman empire, and Roman imperial power is under threat. New religious movements interact, or compete, with the traditional religion, and the leaders of Christian churches have new roles in the community. New ideas of a life committed to God challenge the old ideals of service to family, city, and country. Power shifts to new locations, so that in 410 a Roman emperor based in Ravenna takes no action to rescue the city of Rome from the barbarians, and his co-emperor, based in Constantinople, is not affected. New opportunities for talent open up, in military and civil service, in public speaking and in the church, but old families, old money, and traditional education and values, still keep their prestige. No wonder late antiquity has fascinated European and North American scholars in the late 20th and early 21st centuries.

What, then, is 'late' about late antiquity? 'Antiquity' means, vaguely, 'ancient times'. It often means classical antiquity, the centuries when Greece and Rome set the standard of culture: 'classical' comes from Latin *classicus*, which means 'first class' in the Roman social system. Classical culture remains inspirational, but in late antiquity the classical world changed. By the 3rd century AD, the Roman empire still extended from Britain to Ethiopia and from Spain to the Euphrates, but the city of Rome was no longer its centre, and it was no longer governed by the Senate and People of Rome. In the late 1st century BC, when Augustus established himself as in practice the first emperor of Rome, he was careful to hold office in traditional Roman style, as consul with a colleague. He consulted the Senate, which was an advisory council of experienced politicians, most of them members of rich and influential families. He gave important posts to senators, and when he was not on military campaigns, he lived in Rome. He liked to be called *princeps*, 'first citizen', and refused to be called *dominus*, 'Lord', the word used by slaves to address their masters.

Some historians think that late antiquity begins when 'principate' gives way to 'dominate': that is, when the emperor was openly acknowledged as master, or even as Lord and God, and when freeborn Roman citizens, if they were of low status, were liable to physical punishments which were once reserved for slaves. This happened by the late 2nd century AD, if not sooner. In late antiquity, years could pass before the emperor visited Rome, for his decisions had the force of law. They did not require authorization at Rome by the Senate and People, whose political support was no longer necessary. Some important posts still went to members of the urban Roman elite, but the emperor's power openly depended on soldiers, and on a second army of administrators, the civil service (*militia civilis*), who, like the soldiers, wore the military belt. More bureaucracy – or more efficient administration, depending on your perspective – is another characteristic of late antiquity.

From the late 1st century AD, the city of Rome lost its importance as a centre of government: emperors could be made elsewhere than Rome, and often spent long periods away from Rome. Half way down the Italian peninsula, on a river which flooded, and some distance inland from a harbour vulnerable to storms and silting, Rome was not an effective military base for wars outside Italy. Instead, emperors moved with their courts and armies to meet the next immediate threat, or stayed for a time in cities which were better placed: Antioch in Syria, Constantinople on the Bosphorus, Sirmium (Zagreb) on the Danube, Ravenna and Milan on the north Italian plain, Trier on the Rhine. As those locations show, the major military threats came from the east and the north. To the east, there was always a great power across the Euphrates river, sometimes united under a forceful dynasty, and sometimes fragmented by rebellion and infighting. From the 3rd to the 7th centuries, the Sassanian dynasty, which began as a Persian revolt, ruled an empire which extended over present-day Iran, Iraq, Afghanistan, the Persian Gulf, and the Caucasus. This Persian empire came to be united by a common language, currency, and administration, and by an official religion, called Zoroastrianism after its prophet Zoroaster or Mazdaism after the deity Ahura Mazda. Roman emperors sometimes accepted coexistence with Persia, but sometimes tried pre-emptive strikes or wars of conquest, often in alliance with rebels against the ruling dynasty; and sometimes Persian emperors invaded Roman territory and defeated Roman armies.

The threat from the north came not from a rival empire, but from warrior peoples who pushed into Roman territory. Romans called them barbarians, and tried to identify their shifting groups as Goths and Vandals, Huns and Avars and Slavs. Emperors sometimes tried to fight off or buy off the barbarians, and sometimes encouraged them to join the Roman army and to settle on Roman lands. Threats from the east and the north were as old as the empire, but in late antiquity the threats became stronger. In the 5th century, Roman rule in western Europe gave way to barbarian kingdoms in France and Spain and Italy and North Africa. Here, Roman and barbarian cultural traditions, and different interpretations of Christianity, became markers of political and ethnic loyalties.

1. The enemy: the captive emperor Valerian bows before the Persian king Shapur I, late 3rd century

In the 7th century, the Arabs of the eastern deserts united, and both Roman and Persian rule in the Near East fell back before the advance of Islam. The Mediterranean was no longer 'our sea' united by Roman rule. Its southern and eastern coasts were ruled first from Damascus, then from a new Arab capital at Baghdad; its northern coast was divided among barbarian kingdoms; and Byzantium continued to defend Roman territory in Greece and the Balkans against attacks from the east and the north.

Decline and fall?

Rome is the great example of the decline and fall of an empire, and Edward Gibbon's masterpiece, *The History of the Decline and Fall of the Roman Empire* (1776–88), made the concept very familiar. Historians now ask whether it is right. Did Rome fall, or did it survive? Gibbon composed his history in three sections: from the emperor Trajan, based in Rome, in the early 2nd century, to the fall of the western empire in the late 5th century; from the

6

emperor Justinian, based in Constantinople, in the 6th century, to Charlemagne, King of the Franks and Holy Roman Emperor, who united most of western Europe in the 9th century; and from the 9th century to the end of Byzantium, when the Turks took Constantinople in 1453.

In the west, from the late 5th century onwards, Europe was ruled by non-Roman kings, but Roman culture survived in law and literature, philosophy and theology, and in the traditions of the church. Latin, not Frankish or Vandal or Gothic, is the basis of the Romance, that is Roman, languages of Europe. In the east, despite great loss of territory, a Greek-speaking Roman empire continued for centuries. We call it Byzantium, but that name was given by a 16th-century scholar, Hieronymus Wolf. Its people called themselves Romans and Muslim historians called them Rûm. 'Rome' is the name of a city and of an empire. 'Byzantium', now the name of an empire, was the name of the Greek town which the emperor Constantine, in the early 4th century, made into New Rome Constantinople, 'city of Constantine'. Some people like to hear its present-day name, Istanbul, as *eis tēn polin*, Greek for 'to the city'; Roman administrative systems continued even under Turkish rule. So there is a case for saying that Roman culture survived the fall of imperial power in the west, and that both culture and imperial power continued in the east.

Did Rome fall, or was it pushed? Gibbon thought that the Roman empire achieved a high point of civilization in the mid-2nd century, and that the chief cause of decline was the impact of 'barbarism and religion' on the Roman character. In his view, barbarians were undisciplined, religion was intolerant, and Christian religion valued idle and unproductive people who became monks and nuns. Gibbon famously wrote, 'It was at Rome, on the 15th of October, 1764, as I sat musing amid the ruins of the Capitol, while the barefooted friars were singing vespers in the Temple of Jupiter, that the idea of writing the decline and fall of the city first started to my mind.' But Franciscan friars, committed to personal poverty and to support for the poor, do not necessarily represent decline from the days when an emperor climbed the Capitoline Hill, whose temples were the symbol of Roman power, to perform blood sacrifice to Jupiter Best and Greatest. Some historians have suggested that so far from undermining Rome, barbarian vigour and Christian commitment transformed the classical heritage, and were themselves transformed by classical culture. Others again have pointed to the difficulty of defining Romans against barbarians, or pagans against Christians, because Romans and barbarians and pagans and Christians differed among themselves, and because many people who were legally Roman were also Greek by culture, Christian by religion, barbarian by ancestry, or a mixture, in a hybrid civilization.

But perhaps all this definition, and all this concern for culture and ways of thinking, is a distraction from the factors which determine the experience of most people. Perhaps Rome was pushed to a tipping point, in the west and in the east, by civil war which diverted resources from wars against external enemies, and Roman rule ended because Roman armies lost too many wars. War devoured men and crops, devastated the tax base which sustained the armies, disrupted trade, and took bullion out of circulation. There was neither the labour force nor the technology to bring marginal or abandoned land into cultivation. Food crises and epidemics were interrelated, just as they are now. Armies take food, and soldiers are vulnerable to epidemics because they are crowded together as they move into unfamiliar territory. People living close to starvation are also vulnerable to epidemics, and new techniques of skeletal analysis have shown that malnutrition was endemic. The poor are always vulnerable to the rich, who own the land, buy up food as prices rise, or simply take it; and when food has to be imported, with the imports come new epidemics.

In principle, as Christian preachers pointed out, the rich could have helped the poor by charitable giving, but some problems were just too much for human goodwill and resources. Historians in late antiquity wrote about intense cold, years without sun, tidal waves, earthquakes, and plagues. In 536, according to a 12th-century chronicler, 'for a year and a half the sun was dark. It shone for only four hours a day, and even that light was feeble. Fruit did not ripen, and wine tasted of sour grapes.' Historians were expected to write for effect, and the set-piece account of disaster was part of their repertoire, but in late antiquity they may have needed it. There is increasing evidence, from tree rings and ice cores, for an environmental catastrophe around 535, with a global fall in temperature and changed patterns of rainfall. The cause may have been a comet, or a meteor strike, or a dust veil produced by a massive volcanic eruption somewhere in south-east Asia, greater even than the eruption of Krakatoa in 1883. Cold, wet, sunless seasons caused crop failure and prompted population shifts among nomadic peoples, in the steppes and in Arabia, who had lost their usual sources of supply. Bubonic plague reached Constantinople in 542, perhaps carried by rats on trading ships. Together with major wars, it caused a serious fall in population, and it recurred through the next two centuries.

Look at the archaeology of western Europe, not at the written texts and visual arts of high culture, and you find Roman towns hurriedly fortified, civic buildings and aqueducts not maintained, makeshift housing in the grand public spaces, and great houses divided up for apartments and workshops. Pottery styles are crude and foodstuffs are limited, because people were restricted to local resources. But evidence of decline is not found everywhere at the same time: some cities prospered, some villages expanded, and conditions in the eastern Mediterranean differed from those in the west. It all depends on what you are looking for, where, and when.

Who belongs where?

Every year of research extends the boundaries of late antiquity. Travel, war, and trade connected regions which were never ruled by Rome, and where people learned Latin or Greek as a second or third language, if they learned them at all. Texts and artefacts challenge the Mediterranean perspective of Roman authors: ideas travelled with the amber trade along the Danube and with the silk trade across central Asia, and monks smuggled silkworm eggs from China to Constantinople. Platonist philosophers visited the Middle East, there were Jewish and Christian academies in Persia, and the religion taught by Mani in 3rd-century Mesopotamia moved westward in a form which connected with Christianity and eastward in a form which connected with Buddhism.

In time, the boundaries are even more fluid. Late antiquity may start in the mid-2nd century with Marcus Aurelius, the philosopher emperor who wrote his 'Notes to Self', the *Meditations*, in his tent by the Danube on campaign against the northern barbarians. It may start at the beginning of the 3rd century, when the death of the soldier emperor Septimius Severus was followed by decades of civil war; or at the end of the 3rd century with Diocletian, who reorganized the empire; or in the early 4th century with Constantine, the first openly Christian emperor. It may end around 800, when a new range of sources becomes available: in the west from the Carolingian dynasty which fostered Latin literature and scholarship, and in the east from the Abbasid caliphate, based in Baghdad, which fostered Arabic literature. But 800 is not a significant break in the history of Byzantium, and in all contexts, whenever one historian finds a watershed or a rupture, another finds the stream that flows through and the evidence for continuity.

Historians vary in what they recognize in past societies and what they find most important or most interesting in human life: basic needs for food and security; political and social organization; military and technical developments; beliefs about human nature and about the gods; culture and creativity. The study of late antiquity reveals strong feelings about all of these, especially about religion as a force for good or bad. In *City of God*, Augustine offered his own perspective on human history. He saw a fundamental problem: in a world created good, but flawed by human sin, people seek to dominate, to do it their way. Latin *imperium* means the power to give orders; empire is large-scale domination. Without justice, empires are gangs, which survive by obeying their leaders and their rules for sharing out loot. They have their uses, because social order, and sometimes force, are needed to maintain imperfect human peace. But no empire has a special status, and it does not greatly matter who is in charge and which customs and language prevail. Roman culture heroes put the public interest before their own because they wanted empire and glory, and they got it.

> They were honoured by almost all peoples; they imposed the laws of their empire on many peoples; today they are glorious in literature and history among almost all peoples. They have no grounds for complaint against the justice of the supreme and true God: they have their reward.

In the time of Augustus, Virgil wrote the *Aeneid*, in which Anchises, father of Aeneas, proclaims Rome's mission statement to 'have empire over the peoples, spare the subject, and fight down the proud', and Jupiter declares that he has given Rome 'empire without end'. In late antiquity, schoolboys still read Virgil, but Augustine questioned those claims to endless empire.

Augustine died in 430, when his town was under siege by the barbarian Vandals, who had crossed from Spain. Historians at the time said that the Vandals were extremely cruel, especially to Christian clergy whose theology was different from their own. But these barbarians established a North African kingdom which lasted for a century, until the emperor Justinian sent troops against them from Constantinople. 'Vandal' now means someone who destroys culture, but according to Procopius, who wrote the history of Justinian's wars, the Vandals took to Roman luxury in the rich territory they had conquered: they had baths and wore

11

silk, made gardens and dined well, and were entertained by dancers and chariot races. The Vandals maintained the city of Carthage, built churches, and commissioned Latin poems. Their language of administration was Latin, and their African Latin may have returned to Spain as the Arab invasions of the 7th century pushed westward. They even had problems of their own with local *barbari* who came to be known as Berbers. Procopius tells a story of the last Vandal king, Gelimer, besieged by Justinian's troops in the Atlas mountains. He was offered an honourable surrender, but asked instead for a loaf of bread, which he had not eaten for months; a sponge to treat a swollen eye; and a lyre, because he was a skilled player and wanted to perform an ode he had composed on his misfortune. When he did surrender, and met the Roman commander, he laughed uncontrollably. Those present said that he was not distraught: this was the only possible response to the changes of fortune. Gelimer was taken to Constantinople, where he walked in chains in the triumphal procession which offered Justinian the spoils of the Vandal kingdom. He did not weep, but repeated a Bible verse from the book of Ecclesiastes, 'Vanity of vanities, all is vanity'. The next verse is 'What profit hath a man of all his labour which he taketh under the sun?'

Late antiquity saw conflict of values and competition for resources, but also recognition of common ground. Augustine, who died in danger, recognized the importance of the Roman empire as a force for peace and unity, but insisted that Rome was the Romans, not buildings and walls and temporary rulers. Empires come and go, rulers are good or bad, but two cities endure. We cannot see them, because citizenship depends on what you love, not on birth or political allegiance or membership of institutions, including the church. One is the city of this world, the community of all who want what they want. The other, the community of all who want what God wants, is the city of God. Who belongs where? We shall not know until the end of time.

Chapter 2
Running the empire

Peace and order were the basic duties of Roman government, so that people could get on with their lives untroubled by invasions and civil wars and crime. Late antiquity is often taken to start with the emperor Diocletian (reigned 284–305), who did impose peace and order, after a long period of disruption with an exceptionally fast turnover of emperors. Diocletian's enemies said that his parents had been slaves; the army was his route to power, first as a successful soldier, then as leader of a military coup and victor in civil war. This may help to explain why, as emperor, he was surrounded by the ceremonial reverence of a court. He spent very little time in Rome. His armies were commanded by professional soldiers, and his advisory council was staffed by senior civil servants, who were also in the *militia* ('the service'), not by senators from great Roman families. The council was called a 'consistory', literally a 'standing' committee, because it was not proper to sit in the presence of the emperor. Diocletian greatly increased the number of soldiers, and recognized that he had to pay for them. Like all managers with limited options, he restructured and standardized and tried to balance income and expenditure. Like all managers, he found that some problems persisted: too little cash, too many barbarians, and no easy way to increase productivity.

2. The emperor, his officials, and his people: Arch of Constantine, Rome

The Roman empire was very big, and communication was slow. People travelling on official business could get permits to use the 'public transport' system, which required local officials to keep changes of horses at staging-posts along the major routes. This made travel faster, but was not much help in winter when storms made sailing dangerous and roads were blocked by snow or mud or flooding. Diocletian tried to improve efficiency by reorganizing administrative regions. Church tradition preserves their Greek name, 'diocese', and the Latin name 'vicar' (*vicarius*) for the local deputy of a senior official. Regions had a military commander (*dux*, 'leader', hence 'duke') and a civil governor (*comes*, 'companion' of the emperor, hence 'count'). Separating troops from law and finance made both tasks manageable. It also reduced the risk of rebellion when a commander, his troops, or people in his region, decided that he could do a better job than the emperor. Diocletian, himself a successful rebel, tried to stabilize the situation with a tetrarchy ('four-man rule') of two senior generals, one based in the east and one in the west, with two junior generals in training to take over from them. This worked for a while, and Diocletian, exceptionally, was able to retire to his home town on the east coast of the Adriatic, instead of dying on the job. But military power remained decisive, succession crises and civil war persisted, and power was often divided among co-emperors.

Some emperors achieved sole power. Among them was Constantine, who in the second half of his 30-year reign (307–37) added Rome's eastern Mediterranean territories to his western base, and developed a new capital at Constantinople which diverted resources from Rome. His enemies said that his own son was among the rebels he killed, so he had to be Christian, because nobody else would forgive him. At the end of the 4th century, Theodosius I (379–95) dominated his co-emperors, but his sons had different spheres of influence, one in the Greek-speaking east, the other in the Latin-speaking west, which extended into the Balkans and along the North African coast. This was probably not a long-term plan, but the pattern continued. From 395, the western empire lost territory outside Italy, and after 476 Italy too was ruled by non-Romans, though the Senate and the Pope, both based in Rome, continued to have influence. But the eastern empire survived, and in the 530s Justinian was able to reconquer some western territory from Vandals in North Africa and from Ostrogoths in Italy. Throughout these changes, Latin was an imperial, but not a global, language. Greek-speakers thought it was an inferior dialect of Greek, and saw no need to learn it unless they wanted a career in the imperial civil service: Latin remained the official language of law until Justinian, in the 530s, began to issue laws in Greek. For Latin-speakers, fluent Greek was a sign of culture, but some emperors needed an interpreter. Even when they spoke the same language, it was not in practice easy for two emperors and their officials to have the same priorities or even to keep each other informed.

While an emperor retained power, he was at the top of the political system. Official rhetoric and visual imagery presented the earthly ruler as exceptionally close to the divine power which rules the universe. Diocletian, having no family claim to power, said he was emperor by the will of the gods, and took the additional name Jovius, 'belonging to Jupiter'. Later historians said that those who approached him had to kiss the hem of his purple military cloak, as if he were a Persian king. Imperial purple was the most expensive form of a dye made from the *murex* shellfish; it was reserved for imperial use, and by the late 4th century actors were forbidden to wear purple on stage, even when playing the part of a king.

The special status of the emperor is shown on a heavy silver plate (it weighs over 15 kilograms) commemorating the tenth regnal year of Theodosius I, in 388. The emperor, depicted in high relief, presents letters of authorization to an official who is half his size. The hands of the official are respectfully veiled to receive the gift, and the heads of Theodosius and his two co-emperors are surrounded by a nimbus, a representation of radiance like a halo. Everything about the emperor was 'sacred': there were chamberlains in charge of his 'sacred bedchamber', grants from his treasury were 'sacred largesses', his administrators worked in 'sacred departments', and his 'sacred letters' were received with formal veneration. Then, of course, business proceeded as usual. One 3rd-century papyrus preserves a hurried message to an agent: the divine fortune of our masters has ordered devaluation of the sestertius, so, quick, sell out Italian currency and buy whatever is available.

Did anyone seriously believe that the emperor was especially close to the divine? In the 330s, the astrologer Firmicus Maternus claimed that the emperor was not bound by the decrees of fate, as ordinary human beings are, so it was not possible to cast his horoscope. Firmicus may have written this because investigating the emperor's horoscope was a capital offence: it could only mean that you wanted to know when he would die. In the late 4th century, the orator Themistius drew on a long tradition of argument, deriving from Plato, that the best rulers are those who

3. The emperor above his officials: ceremonial silver dish, late 4th century

understand the nature of the good. The emperor, he said, is 'animate law', the living representative of the divine law which governs the universe and which should be reflected in human law; so the emperor is above human law and can mitigate its harshness.

The emperor could indeed intervene to show mercy, or could change the law, but some legal experts thought that he should submit to the present state of the law. Did anyone, including the orator, believe the claims made in speeches of praise? Augustine thought not. 'How wretched I was on the day when I was preparing to declaim the praises of the emperor, in which I would tell many lies, and would win approval from people who knew I was lying!' He was then professor of rhetoric at Milan, and the emperor, Valentinian II, was about ten years old, but any trained orator knew what could be said about the splendid ancestry and

17

exceptional promise of someone who had yet to achieve anything. If there was no ancestry, the orator could refer to the favour of the gods. Rhetoric, in such ceremonial performances, was not expected to persuade: it was used to reaffirm consensus, as at party conferences.

Some emperors were more relaxed and accessible than others, but all were surrounded by servants and courtiers and ceremonial, and so were at risk of being isolated from information. People at court could acquire power, not because they held office, but because they had access to the emperor as family members or personal servants. Women did not hold any official post, or have any official role in decision making, but some had considerable influence through their family status, their property, and their contacts. It is surprising that unofficial power-holders included court eunuchs, as in Persia. Roman law penalized castration as assault, except when it was done for certified medical reasons; this is not surprising, because the person castrated not only lost the legal and social status of a male, he was likely to die from shock or from infection. Most procedures were carried out on non-Romans and outside Roman territory. Eunuchs were doubly suspect as unmanly and un-Roman, so why were they household servants of the Roman emperor? There are two obvious advantages: pregnancy would not result from affairs with women of the imperial family, and eunuchs were personally dependent on the emperor because they did not have Roman social and family ties. But they could have godchildren or favourites, and they could transfer their loyalty to a rival. Perhaps it was also an advantage that Roman distaste made it easy to blame the eunuchs for whatever went wrong between the emperor and his officials or his people.

The emperor at the games

Because the emperor was isolated, it was very important for him to attend the public games. This showed that he shared the pleasures of ordinary people, and it was their one opportunity to

4. The emperor at the games: late 4th-century carving on the base of an Egyptian obelisk brought to Constantinople

shout slogans he would personally hear. When Constantine made the town Byzantion into 'New Rome Constantinople', one feature he added was the Hippodrome for chariot races, modelled on the Circus Maximus at Rome, with an imperial box and direct access from the palace. Leading charioteers had fan clubs of emotional supporters, as footballers do now. This led to some dramatic clashes between ordinary people and the forces of the state.

In 390, at Thessalonica, the military commander Botheric arrested a popular charioteer, and was killed in the resultant riot. The death of an imperial official was a very serious offence, and Theodosius I ordered his troops to take action. Many innocent people were killed, and to make matters worse, Botheric was a Goth. He was a Christian serving in the Roman army, but Christian Goths were usually Arian. This theology, named for the theologian Arius of Alexandria, held that Jesus Christ, as Son of God, is greater than all created beings, but derives his being from the Father. It was not acceptable to 'Nicene' Christians who followed the Council of Nicaea (325) in holding that the Son is 'of the same being as' the Father, and who claimed to be the Catholic, that is the universal (Greek *katholikos*), church. Few chariot fans could have explained the difference, but in Thessalonica and elsewhere, it meant Them and Us. So a Catholic emperor was responsible for the deaths of innocent Catholic Romans, in reprisal for the death of an Arian Goth.

What happened next can be interpreted in two ways: the most powerful man in the Roman world yields to the spiritual authority of a bishop, or a politically minded bishop offers the emperor a solution to his problem. At the time of the reprisals, the court was at Milan, whose bishop Ambrose was a Roman aristocrat and former governor of the region. Generations of historians accepted the version of events he wrote to his sister: Theodosius was responsible for the deaths of innocent people, and Ambrose refused him communion until he did penance. The National Gallery in London has Van Dyck's copy of a famous painting by Rubens, in which Ambrose, in full episcopal robes, bars from his cathedral a bare-headed Theodosius and his restive military escort. It seems a pity to spoil the story, but more sceptical historians see the ex-governor Ambrose as offering a 'repentance opportunity', which solved the problem of Thessalonica and allowed Theodosius to present himself as a pious emperor. Later emperors seem not to have accepted the principle that even an emperor was under the spiritual authority of the church.

Ambrose could not solve the wider problem of fan clubs, the 'circus factions' who chanted for their team and fought rival supporters. They were easily mobilized to support one political leader or religious group against another, and easily identified by the colours of their preferred team: red, white, blue, green. Blues and Greens were especially active in Constantinople in the late 5th and early

6th centuries, and their most spectacular conflict was the 'Nika Riot' of 532, ten days that ended in massacre. It began when the city prefect took action against rioters, arresting seven ringleaders and executing five. One Blue and one Green somehow escaped, and at the next races, the crowd appealed to the emperor to pardon them. Justinian, seated in his imperial box, did not respond, and they rioted again. Chanting 'Nika', 'Win!', as they did for their teams, they stormed and burned the prefect's headquarters.

Still Justinian did not respond, and the demands became political: dismiss the city prefect and two other powerful officials, John the Cappadocian, who was charged with reforming administration, and Tribonian, who headed the commission to codify Roman law. Justinian, apparently, conceded this, but riot and arson continued, and he sent in the troops. When that failed, he made a public appearance in the hippodrome on a Sunday, holding a copy of the Gospels in an appeal to religious feeling. This too failed. Rival candidates for emperor were put forward, and there were rumours that Justinian had fled. The historian Procopius developed a splendid scene in which Justinian's wife Theodora pointed out that they had money and ships available for escape, but 'royalty makes a fine shroud'. The riot was suppressed with great violence, loss of life, and destruction of property; and Justinian began a rebuilding programme which included the great domed church of Hagia Sophia, dedicated five years later. Was it a riot waiting to happen, a riot which could have been defused by a more skilful emperor, a riot exploited by political rivals or opponents of Justinian's reform programme? Nobody knows. Centuries after Justinian, representatives of the Blues and Greens were integrated into Byzantine court ceremonials.

Civil servants

Between the exalted emperor and the people who could only shout slogans at him, or his officials, was an army of administrators. Running the Roman empire meant inspecting and reporting, keeping watch for disaffection, dealing with enquiries and petitions and embassies, drafting and publicizing regulations and laws, collecting taxes in money and kind, paying the army and the civil service. The most senior officials were very powerful. 'Praetorian prefects' of the east and west were commanders in chief, so called because they were in charge at the *praetorium*, that is, HQ. 'Masters of the offices' were in charge of the various *officia*, literally 'responsibilities', that is, departments of the civil service. These departments had subdivisions called *scrinia*, literally 'book-boxes', or bureaux. They used a distinctive 'celestial script' to discourage forgery of official documents. Regional governors also had staff. Some local administration was done by councils (*curiae*) of landowners, but they were always short of members because service was a major financial burden. Members of the imperial civil service were excused local service, and that made the career path even more attractive. Some people were exempted because they already made a contribution to the community, for example as publicly funded teachers and doctors. When Constantine added Christian clergy to the list of exemptions, there was, allegedly, a flood of new vocations, so that he had to backtrack and insist that churches should not choose people who had obligations to their councils unless the obligation was accepted by someone else.

Some people pleaded poverty, which did not mean that they were destitute, only that they were below the property level for compulsory service. Others claimed that they were students, but, then as now, students did not always devote all their time to study. In 370, the Urban Prefect of Rome was told to check up on entry requirements and behaviour:

> The august Emperors Valentinian, Valens and Gratian to Olybrius, prefect of the city. All those who come to the city in the desire to learn shall first of all present to the Chief Tax Officer letters from the provincial judges who gave them permission to come. These letters shall contain the student's town, birth certificate,

and reports of achievement. Second, the students shall declare on arrival which branch of study they propose to follow. Third, the Tax Office shall investigate in detail their places of residence, to ensure that they are devoting their effort to the subject they said they would study. These officials shall also warn the students that they shall all behave in gatherings as befits those who think it right to avoid a bad reputation and bad company, which we consider to be close to crime; nor should they make frequent visits to shows or seek out unseasonable parties. Indeed, we confer on you the power that if anyone does not behave in the city as the dignity of a liberal education requires, he shall be publicly flogged and immediately placed on a boat, expelled from the city and sent home.

Augustine, teaching in Rome, found that students were better behaved than they had been in Carthage; the problem was that they did not pay their tuition fees. But in Athens, the 'dignity of a liberal education' was often at risk. There, town and gown were on such bad terms that teaching had to take place in private lecture rooms. Students of rival teachers fought in the streets, and new arrivals were forcibly recruited at the quayside, for teachers needed student fees even if they had publicly funded posts. Libanius, a leading teacher at Antioch, knew everyone who was anyone, and his immense correspondence includes references and recommendations for generations of students. He complained that his assistant teachers could barely afford a staff of three slaves, who despised the poverty of their owners.

Most students could afford the time and money for higher education, but Prohaeresius, who became a famous teacher of rhetoric, reached Athens with one cloak, one shabby tunic, and a few threadbare blankets, shared with a friend. They took it in turns to stay in bed under the blankets or wear the tunic and cloak to lectures. At the other end of the economic range was a student remembered by his contemporary Gregory, later bishop of Nazianzus, as odd and uncoordinated, eager but confused, with a straggly beard and a prominent Adam's apple. This was the future emperor Julian, who after years of isolation was finally permitted to go to Athens. The emperors acknowledged such hard-working students:

> Those who do work industriously at their professions may stay in Rome until their twentieth year; but after that time, anyone who does not return of his own accord must be sent home in disgrace by the watchfulness of the Prefecture. So that these concerns are not perfunctorily treated, Your High Sincerity shall instruct the Tax Office to compile a monthly record of who has come from where and who, because their time is up, must return to Africa or another province; with the exception of those who are assigned to the obligations of guilds. Let such documents be sent every year to the departments of Our Mildness, so that we may judge from the achievements and training of each person whether and when we need them.

This section of their letter illustrates two important aspects of late antique society. One is a rather charming manifestation of concern for rank: formal modes of address, like 'Your Majesty' or 'Your Excellency', but deploying a much wider range of abstract nouns to show the characteristics expected of the author and the addressee. The other is constraint, or attempted constraint. Most students were members of the social elite, and were needed for service on local councils; members of trade guilds were required to provide essential services. Romans still wanted bread and circuses, so people born into the guild of bakers could not marry out; shipowners could inherit an obligation to transport the grain for subsidized bread at Rome or Constantinople; and actors, born into public entertainment, could not escape the legal disadvantages of their degraded social status. In 371, Christian emperors conceded that performers could not be recalled to the stage if they made an unexpected recovery after deathbed baptism; but it had to be shown that they really were expected to die, and that the clergy approved of the baptism. Hierarchy and constraint seems an ominous combination, but in practice, there were many examples of social mobility; and there were not enough inspectors to check on all the students and bakers and stage performers in the empire, or to prevent tenant farmers from moving away from land which they had agreed to cultivate or where they were registered for tax. The laws which attempt to restrict movement are a response to complaints.

Late antique bureaucracy often gets a bad press. Much to the annoyance of present-day historians, 'Byzantine' connotes obscure political intrigue or complex bureaucratic process. This may be a consequence of late antique history-writing: for many ancient authors, history consisted of manoeuvres and shifting alliances within the imperial household, just as for many present-day authors of political memoirs, history consists of politicians and civil servants in the Whitehall village or the Beltway. But bureaucrats gathered the information which was needed to run the empire, and to achieve some fairness in the administration of resources and of justice.

Equity

Diocletian ordered a new census to find out how many people lived in the Roman empire, what land they owned, and what it could be expected to produce. These are the most obvious ways to tax people, and tax levels could be adjusted for a fixed period in accordance with the current need for troops. But the system had to be flexible, because marginal land left fallow, or unpredictable bad harvests, or bad weather, or epidemics, or war, greatly reduced the amount that could be collected in money or kind. In theory, local landowners on city councils were required to make up the shortfall, but they too were affected by these problems. They used their own rhetorical training, or asked their local teacher of rhetoric, to beg the emperor or the regional governor for tax remission.

Diocletian also tried to stabilize and revalue the currency which was used for the payment of money taxes, and for the salaries of soldiers and civil servants. In principle, Rome had gold, silver, and copper (or copper alloy) coins, in a consistent relationship. In practice, the metal content varied. This did not matter if the face value of the coin was accepted, but in troubled times, people were more likely to hoard coins with a higher gold or silver content. Some local trade could continue without currency, but prices went up when the coinage was debased. Diocletian tried to halt inflation, and to reduce the effect of supply and demand, with a price edict which fixed the maximum price for a very wide range of goods, from basic foodstuffs to half-silk underwear with purple stripes to lions for public entertainment. It also set charges for transport over specific routes, and determined the standard wage for jobs ranging from sewer cleaner to teacher of rhetoric. Death was the penalty for taking goods off the market or otherwise breaking the law. The edict was displayed throughout the empire, and fragments have been found in over forty places.

The price edict begins with a fine example of late antique legal rhetoric, designed to show the context for the decree and to convince people that it is right. Peace is achieved, thank the gods, and the barbarians are destroyed; now peace must be protected by justice, because, shocking though it is, some people are just out to make a profit.

> If self-restraint could check the ravages of greed, which rages without an end in sight, without respect for the human race, pursuing its own gain and increase not only every year and month and day but every hour and minute; if the general welfare could endure without disturbance this licence for riotous behaviour which does it so much harm; there would perhaps appear to be scope for keeping quiet and pretending it was not happening, in the hope that general forbearance would modify this appalling and monstrous situation. But the one desire of this untamed madness is to have no love for common humanity, and among the dishonest and arrogant it is almost a religious principle of greed, which grows and swells with sudden surges, to desist only when forced, not by choice, from rending the fortune of all.

This, and much more, was engraved on stone, but it did not last for long. In several places, the stone was recycled, or even smashed to pieces.

Late antique bureaucrats are also accused of being out to make a profit. They had usually paid money to get a post, their salaries were not enough to live on, and there were no pensions; so extra payments were routine, and some official documents specify the expected level. At Timgad in North Africa, during the brief reign of the emperor Julian, the governor put up an inscription in the marketplace, giving the rates for different services in bushels of wheat or the money equivalent. Clearly, he did not regard this as encouragement of bribery. It could be argued that, like university tuition fees, this system charged only the people who wanted the service. At least they knew what it would cost, and access to service would otherwise have depended even more on contacts and exchange of favours.

Getting access to people in power is never easy:

> It is often said of me, 'Why is he going to that *potestas* [power]? What does a bishop want with that *potestas*?' But you all know that your needs make me go where I do not want to go, and watch, and stand at the door, and wait while worthy and unworthy people go in, and be announced, and finally get in, and put up with snubs, and ask, and sometimes succeed and sometimes go sadly away.

Augustine's status as bishop did not get him privileged access. He used contacts when he had them, but there is no evidence that he used money. Cyril of Alexandria, a much more political bishop in a much richer diocese, provides one of the most spectacular examples of bribery. In 430, he sent 'blessings' to members of the imperial family, officials, and other influential persons in Constantinople, to ensure that they would support his theological position, rather than that of his opponent Nestorius. A letter to Cyril's agents reveals the importance of unofficial power-holders. The wife of the praetorian prefect of the east was offered 100 pounds of gold, the same amount that was given to two senior officials. Chryseros, a eunuch in charge of the sacred bedchamber, was opposed to Cyril, so he was offered double: 200 pounds of gold; six large and four medium tapestries; four large carpets and eight cushions; six each of table-cloths, large and small woven hangings, and stools; twelve throne covers, four large curtains, four thrones and four stools of ivory; six Persian drapes, six large ivory plaques, and six ostrich eggs. Charitable modern historians suggest that Cyril sincerely believed he was ensuring correct doctrine and peace in the church.

Connections and favours were always important, but some of the evidence comes from legislation which sought to prevent bribery and to encourage whistleblowers:

Emperor Constantine to the provincials: The rapacious hands of officials shall stop at once; they shall stop, I say; for if they do not stop when warned, they shall be cut off with swords. The judge's curtain [which screened access to his room] shall not be for sale. Entrance shall not be bought; his private office shall not be notorious for competing bids; the mere sight of the governor shall not come at a price; the ears of the judge shall be open equally to the poorest and to the rich. Introduction by the Head of Office shall be free from extortion; the assistants of the heads of office shall not exert pressure on litigants; the intolerable assaults of the centurions and other officials, who demand small or great sums, shall be crushed; the insatiable greed of those who supply court records to disputants shall be moderated. Let the industry of the governor keep constant watch so that nothing shall be taken from a litigant by these kinds of people.

If the governor did not see what was happening at every level of judicial process, victims of extortion could give him information, and if he did not take action, they could complain to higher authority. Legislation, administration, and official scrutiny might actually help people who were not in a position to work the system, or who wanted to abide by the rules. There is also some evidence for attempts to reduce and simplify bureaucracy. Julian ordered cutbacks at court and in the number of inspectors, but with little effect. Almost two centuries later, Justinian carried out a major reorganization, including the use of Greek for legislation in the eastern empire. John of Cappadocia, his new reforming appointment, was widely unpopular, especially with traditional civil servants who disliked the arrival of the accountants. But perhaps if he had succeeded, 'Byzantine' would now connote efficient and transparent administration.

Chapter 3
Law and welfare

Peace and order cannot be maintained without some use of force, but late antiquity is notorious for state-sanctioned violence. Christian emperors issued laws which threaten atrocious punishments. Civil governors, in their role as judges, were authorized to use torture on suspects and even on witnesses, and in treason cases, rank was no protection. How could Christian officials reconcile such extreme uses of force with Christian teaching on love of neighbour and on returning good for evil? How, on the other hand, could they counter the argument that Christian ethics are incompatible with running an empire, that turning the other cheek is not an adequate response to barbarian invasion, and that 'do not return evil for evil' goes against the principles of justice? Augustine wrote that his opponents asked 'Who would allow something to be taken from him by an enemy? Who would not wish to return evil, by right of war, to someone who pillages a Roman province?'

Augustine did not, as is often supposed, invent the concept of just war. In the late 1st century BC, Cicero formulated Roman tradition: war is just when it resists aggression against one's country or its allies, or reclaims what was taken by aggression, but unprovoked aggression is unjust. A fragment of his philosophical dialogue *Republic* remarks that by defending their allies, the Romans have conquered the world, but without the context we do not know how much irony was intended. Augustine had to go beyond Cicero, because 'thou shalt not kill' is one of the Ten Commandments, and some Christians think it requires pacifism. Augustine agreed with those who interpret it as 'thou shalt not murder'. He distinguished murder from lawful killing, which is permissible provided that it is done on the orders of the duly authorized power, and provided that it is not motivated by anger, but seeks to protect the innocent from criminals and enemies. He saw the danger that rulers might believe they were fighting wars, and taking lives, at God's command: if you think God is telling you to go against the usual rules, he said, you should be very careful.

Augustine recognized that civil as well as military governors must sometimes use force to maintain order, but urged them to think about the force they used. 'The judge may torture the accused so as not to kill an innocent man in ignorance, and it happens through his ignorance that he kills a man who is tortured and innocent'; but he still does not know the truth. Some Roman officials took pride in completing their term of office without ever ordering torture. Some had the instruments of torture displayed on the steps leading up to the judge's tribunal: 'claws' (hooks), the 'pony' (a rack), a brazier for making metal plates red hot. That might be for deterrence, but the judge's official staff included an executioner who was also in charge of torture, and the 'extreme penalties' of Roman law included burning alive and killing by wild animals. Torture and execution were not hidden from view in the cellars of the secret police: they were public spectacles which used legalized violence for retribution and deterrence. Bishops were expected to plead for mercy, or at least for punishment to be reduced to beating with rods, which was less likely to maim or kill than scourging with the lead-weighted *flagellum*. Augustine accepted that social order had a place for the executioner, but still tried to get punishments reduced, even for illegal slave-traders who had kidnapped children, so that the convicted criminals would have time to repent. The local governor responded to one such plea that it was all very well for bishops to ask for mercy, but he had to answer for the crime rate.

Some historians think that Roman government struggled to maintain order: laws were repeated and penalties were harsh, especially for the lower orders (*humiliores,* 'more lowly') who could not afford an advocate or payments to officials, and had no contacts to influence the progress of the case. People of higher social status, the *honestiores* ('more respectable'), were usually safe from physical punishment and cruel forms of execution. But repeated laws may show not failure, but emperors reaffirming zero tolerance of wrongdoing; and brutality and corruption affected Roman law in all periods. We hear more in late antiquity because bishops protested, and because laws threatened punishment for bribe-taking officials, and for judges who were influenced by personal connections instead of judging by the facts and the law.

But how did the judge know the law? He was a civil servant, not a legal expert. In principle, all inhabitants of the Roman empire were governed by the same laws, and all regional governors were informed of new developments. In practice, local custom was often respected, especially in family matters, and the governor and his legal advisors could not simply look up the law. Legislation, and interpretation by legal experts, had accumulated since the 5th century BC. Emperors created precedents by their responses to queries and petitions, but new laws were not always published throughout the empire. As if that were not enough, Constantine decreed that Christian bishops could decide civil cases, so that people were spared the expense and delays of legal action. There was a well established tradition of using an arbitrator accepted by both parties, but Constantine shocked his civil servants by saying that one party could choose to take the case to the bishop, and that the bishop's decision must be accepted, because bishops, being holy, could discern the truth.

Late antiquity saw repeated attempts to collect, revise, and clarify Roman law. These attempts are very useful to historians, because a law with a date and an addressee shows at least that someone had asked for a response to a problem, even if it does not show that the problem was widespread and that action followed. The *Corpus Iuris Civilis*, literally the 'body of civil law', was compiled on the orders of Justinian in the second and third decades of the 6th century, but collections of laws began three centuries earlier, in the time of the Severan emperors. The Severi were openly *domini*, masters, whose power depended on military force. The historian Cassius Dio (consul in 229) wrote that the last words of Septimius Severus to his sons were 'make the soldiers rich, and the hell with everything else'. But the Severi came from Africa, which had a great tradition of producing advocates, and they also fostered developments in Roman law.

The emperor Marcus Aurelius Severus Antoninus Augustus says: All reasons and reasoning should refer to the divine. So it is right that I too should give thanks to the immortal gods, because they kept me safe when the great conspiracy arose. Now I think this can be done with dignity and as befits the greatness of the gods, if I bring to their sanctuaries all the thousands who have joined my people. I therefore grant to all inhabitants of the earth the citizenship of the Romans…

Marcus Aurelius Severus Antoninus Augustus was usually known as Caracalla, 'Hoodie', from the Celtic-style tunic he liked to wear, but this declaration of 212, the *Constitutio Antoniniana*, carries his formal name. A *constitutio* is a decree affecting the whole empire. Roman policy on citizenship had always been a factor in Roman success. Most Greek states restricted citizenship to those who lived in the city and its surrounding land, so that they could take part in local politics; it followed that people could be citizens of only one city. Rome accepted that citizens could live too far away for participation, and that they could hold both Roman and local citizenship. So there was no conflict of loyalties, and when subject peoples became citizens, their adult males were eligible for service in Roman armies. Many historians have interpreted Caracalla's decree as the culmination of this policy, or even as an idealistic vision of a united empire. But 'all inhabitants of the earth' did not include slaves, who could not be citizens until they were freed, and 'the earth' could not go beyond territory controlled by Rome. Caracalla also doubled the inheritance tax which was paid by Roman citizens to the military treasury, and Cassius Dio, who disliked him, said that his real purpose was to expand the base for taxation and army recruitment.

Caracalla ensured that Roman law applied, in principle, across the world. But how did a Roman governor know what Roman law was? The answer came from Ulpian (d. 223), one of the greatest Roman jurists, that is, experts on law. He came from Tyre in Phoenicia, a multicultural city. Ulpian researched imperial edicts and responses in the archives at Rome, organized them by topic, and wrote a reference book, *The Duty of a Governor*, which combined a collection of laws with discussion of their underlying principles. He rose to be praetorian prefect at Rome, and died there in an outbreak of political violence. At the end of the 3rd century, in the reign of Diocletian, legal experts compiled two more collections of laws. Each was called a 'codex', but these were not 'codes' in the sense of a comprehensive system of law. *Codex* is Latin for a book with pages, as distinct from a book-roll (*volumen*, hence 'volume'); it is much easier to find a reference in a *codex* than in a roll, and the *codex* was increasingly used in late antiquity.

In the 5th century, Theodosius II decided to have legal material organized in a single Code which would exclude error, contradiction, and ambiguity. It would do more than tell his subjects what they must not do: it would tell them how to live their lives. In practice, it was a collection of imperial decrees, starting from 313 in the reign of Constantine, and assuming that all laws were in the name of all emperors who reigned at the time, even if they were not in a position to consult. The compilers worked at Constantinople from 429 to 437. They arranged their material in chronological order under headings, sometimes redistributing a law across different sections, and reducing the length of the text when they could.

Much of the Theodosian Code does not survive, but one 11th-century manuscript preserves the extraordinary account of its welcome, in 438, by the senators at Rome. They chanted 'acclamations', and just as the length of applause at a political conference is recorded now, so the number of acclamations was recorded then. Chanting of slogans, petitions, or approval was a widespread practice. In 438, the Senate began with several standard chants in praise of the emperor, for example 'God gave you to us, God keeps you for us' (27 times). But it is hard to imagine how the chants were orchestrated when the acclamations, following a familiar pattern, changed from praise to specific requests:

> Let many copies be made for the departments! (10 times)
> Let them be kept under seal in the bureaux of state! (20 times)
> So that the laws should not be falsified, let many copies be made!
>   (25 times)
> So that the laws should not be falsified, let all copies be written out!
>   (18 times)
> Let no annotations be added to the copy which is to be made by the
>   *constitutionarii*! (12 times).

They do not even sound catchier in Latin. But they showed the strength of support for these practical measures, and that is why they survived. Five years later, the praetorian prefect sent the record of the meeting to the court at Ravenna, because he wanted confirmation that only the *constitutionarii* were authorized to make copies.

Justinian's project began a century later, in 528. The *Corpus Iuris Civilis* has three parts. The *Institutes* is a legal textbook. The

Digest is an organized collection of authoritative legal opinion, much of it from the three centuries before Diocletian, in which Ulpian is an important presence. The *Codex Justinianus* added some earlier and some later legislation to the material collected in the Theodosian Code. *Novellae*, 'new items' (often confusingly translated 'Novels'), were added later. One of these, dated 545, gives the status of law to the rulings ('canons') of four great church councils: this is the beginning of 'canon law'. Some of the *Novellae* reveal fundamental change in the Roman empire, because they are in Greek, the administrative language of the east, not in Latin, the traditional language of law. In the late 4th century, Libanius complained that his students would not give enough time to Greek rhetoric, because they were off to law school at Berytus (Beirut) to learn Latin and make a career in the imperial service. By the mid-6th century, the balance had shifted, and John the Lydian, in Constantinople, complained that the new generation of civil servants would not give enough time to Latin.

Welfare

Roman government was not expected to take responsibility for welfare, but sometimes acted when social order was at risk. New Rome Constantinople followed the example of Rome in distributing free or subsidized grain – to those entitled, not to those in need – and grain shortages prompted riots. Local governors also responded to emergencies such as floods and earthquakes and famines and epidemics. But they were not expected to provide food and health care for everyone who was affected, and if the emperor sent funds or remitted taxes in a crisis, that was a benefaction, to be acknowledged with public demonstrations of gratitude.

Late antiquity saw charity overtake benefaction as Christianity increased its influence. Benefactors were essential in a society without welfare provision. They funded public buildings, entertainments, and distributions of food or money for their fellow citizens, and sometimes they endowed a funded post for a doctor or teacher. Their reward was public recognition. Augustine asked his patron Romanianus to imagine it:

> Suppose you gave our citizens contests with bears, and spectacles never before seen, and were always greeted by the warmest applause in the theatre; suppose you were praised to the skies by the shouts of foolish people (and of those there are many); suppose the official records of the town declared you, on bronze tablets, to be the patron not only of its citizens but of the neighbourhood; suppose statues were raised, honours flowed in, powers were added which surpassed those of towns [....] Suppose you were proclaimed by dependents, fellow-citizens, local people to be the most kindly, generous, decent, fortunate of men...

People of this kind felt the force of expectation. They had to balance the claims of family members, dependants, and fellow citizens, without giving to the unworthy and without making their household unable to maintain its position. Christians were taught to follow a different principle, in the Jewish tradition of responding to human need, but they too had to consider how much to give. Two works called 'On Duties' make the contrast clear. Cicero, writing in the late 1st century BC for his son Marcus, included discussion of priorities in giving. Ambrose of Milan, writing for his spiritual sons, the clergy, in the late 4th century AD, expected his readers to know about Cicero, but asked different questions. Should we sell church silver to ransom prisoners of war? Ambrose did, but opponents said that he wanted to show his power over the great families whose names were on the silver they donated. Do the teachings of Jesus require us to give all we have? Already in the late 2nd century, Clement of Alexandria, writing on 'The Rich Man's Salvation', had pointed out that a Christian who gives moderately and consistently is more useful than one who gives all he has to the poor, then becomes one more name on the bishop's welfare list.

The bishop as source of support was a late antique innovation. The benefactor used his or her own resources in exchange for honour in the city; the bishop drew on the resources of his congregation, offering in exchange honour in the church, the prayers of the poor, and a reward in heaven. Many bishops encouraged the sustainable gift of endowments for churches and monasteries, which could continue to support the poor by growing food for distribution or renting land to tenants. From the earliest records of the church, deacons (Greek *diakonos*, 'administrator') had specific responsibility for funds and distribution. In the late 4th century, the poet Prudentius wrote on Laurence, a deacon martyred at Rome in the mid-3rd century. The wicked governor demands the treasures of the church, and Laurence asks for time to assemble them. Then he leads in the poor who are supported by the church, saying that these destitute and disabled people are the church's greatest treasure. The governor, furious, has him tied to a gridiron over a slow fire, and the martyr makes his famous joke 'this side's done, turn me over'.

Classical literature had little to say about the poor, but Christian literature insisted on making them visible. In the late 4th century, when crop failures and harsh winters brought famine to Cappadocia in central Asia Minor, Basil bishop of Caesarea preached harrowing sermons. He forced potential donors to imagine the emaciated bodies by the roadside, and the father who cannot feed his children deciding which one to sell into slavery. Basil himself came from a rich family and was able to take practical action. His complex of buildings, at a cross-roads of major routes, provided food, shelter, and medical care for travellers and displaced people. It was called 'Basileias'. *Basileia* is Greek for 'kingdom': was this the kingdom of God in action, or was it a more human kingdom, 'Basil's place'? The local governor felt that Basil's initiative was too much like competition, for officials too were now expected to show concern for the poor. Basil's contemporary Julian, who rejected his Christian upbringing, wrote that the traditional religion must follow the example of Jews and Christians in providing for all those in need. This was not a new departure, Julian claimed, for the great god Zeus watched over strangers and travellers, and Homer offers the example of Eumaeus, the swineherd who gives hospitality to the destitute Odysseus. Christian authors said that Julian appropriated Christian ideas to the point of planning a welfare budget for temples.

By the early 6th century, Christian charitable organization was well established. Justinian and his empress Theodora had many charitable projects. One of these, a refuge for prostitutes, prompted mixed reactions. If there is truth in the stories of Theodora's early life as a showgirl, she knew about the economic and social pressures on the girls who worked the marketplace. A law of Justinian recognized that some prostitutes were sold by deceived or desperate parents when they were scarcely ten years old: for them, the refurbished fortress called Metanoia might indeed be a refuge from clients and pimps. 'Metanoia', 'change of mind', is often translated 'repentance'; for some, 'fresh start' would be appropriate. But according to Procopius, some inhabitants of Metanoia were so desperate to escape that they jumped from the roof into the Bosphorus.

Justinian's legislation shows that gifts and legacies to churches and bishops were frequent, and there were practical problems when money was left 'for the poor', unspecified. In 6th-century Constantinople, there was a range of welfare provision. Babies left on the steps of a church would be cared for in an orphanage. Hospices offered nursing care, and some imperial women showed their Christian commitment by helping with the basic tasks. Hospices were not hospitals providing specialist medical treatment, but Constantinople had *archiatri*, doctors at the top of their profession, and the combination of expertise and a wide range of cases helped to develop medical practice. Laws of the 6th century expected bishops to take an active interest in welfare management, visiting prisons, protecting orphans and foundlings, helping to free slaves who had been forced to work as prostitutes or entertainers, and intervening when officials abused power or mismanaged funds.

Of course, more could have been done to relieve human need. In the late 4th century, John Chrysostom told his congregation in Antioch that they could eliminate starvation in their city: he had no statistics, but he knew about church welfare lists. Basil, fighting famine in Cappadocia, targeted donors with a sermon on Jesus' story of the man whose harvest was too big for his barn. Did he distribute the surplus? No: he said, 'I will pull down my barn, and build bigger barns'. That night he died.

Chapter 4
Religion

Many present-day historians have no religious belief. They may concede that some believers mean well, but they do not see why anyone minds about religion except as politics by other means, or why so much writing about late antiquity is concerned with religion. But editing out religion means editing out the religious change which is one of the most distinctive, and spectacular, features of late antiquity: saints on pillars and monks in the desert; relics venerated and statues destroyed; women enclosed in their rooms or travelling on long-distance pilgrimage; senators initiated into mystery cults and emperors discussing belief statements. Three Christian innovations transformed Roman and post-Roman society: bishops as community leaders, experiments in monastic living, and emperors backing insistence on orthodoxy, that is, right belief (Greek *orthodoxia*). Until the later 20th century, historians living in Christian or post-Christian countries usually focused on Christian doctrine and practice. Now they include Judaism, Islam, the traditional religion which Christians called 'pagan', and more generally the ways in which people thought about their relationship to God and what it meant for how they should live.

In traditional Roman religion, the same people were political and religious leaders. Priesthood was another public office, not a vocation to a life of personal holiness, teaching, and pastoral care.

Priests performed specific rituals, usually once a year, which brought the community together and reaffirmed the protection of the gods. Cities had patron deities and local rituals, but all these deities belonged to the pantheon, that is to 'all gods' considered as a group, and the gods of non-Roman peoples could usually be identified with one of them. Jupiter Dolichenus, for example, was the god of Doliche in Syria. Some Greek and Roman scholars thought that the god of the Jews was the same as Jupiter, but Jews were exceptional in refusing to acknowledge any other god, to the extent that some Jews resisted with violence when non-Jewish rulers tried to impose non-Jewish cults. Most rulers had the sense to recognize that Judaism was an ancient tradition, unusual in that Jews made no image of their god and in that they sacrificed only to one God and only in one temple. In late antiquity, Jews could not sacrifice, because in AD 70 the Romans had destroyed their temple after a major revolt. But some philosophers thought that this made Judaism even more admirable, because gods do not need sacrifice.

Late antiquity saw the remarkable growth of Christianity from a Jewish fringe group to the dominant religion of the Roman empire. Christian bishops became recognized community leaders, who could influence large numbers of people by preaching and by welfare provision, so emperors had good reason to want the support of bishops, and bishops wanted the support of emperors in religious disputes. Preaching could inspire men and women to give up their family and social responsibilities for an ascetic lifestyle, literally a life in training (Greek *askēsis*), and Christian authors spread sensational accounts of those who made this choice. Preaching could also inspire a crowd to demonstrate against religious opponents, whether these were Jews, or pagans, or Christians with different views; and a demonstration which began with chanting processions could end in assault and destruction. Opponents of Athanasius, bishop of Alexandria in the mid-4th century, claimed that he planned to call out the dockers, so that the grain ships could not leave for Rome. It may not have been true, but it was plausible. Athanasius was exiled seven times from Egypt, sometimes for holding theological views which were not then in favour with the emperor, sometimes on charges of violence and embezzlement. Such accusations, standard in Roman oratory, were widely used in Christian polemic.

Gibbon thought that religion, specifically Christian religion, was a major cause of the fall of Rome, because religious communities absorbed the energies of people who could have contributed to the empire, and because religion meant intolerance. People who would have been soldiers or administrators or producers became 'idle mouths'; Christians claimed that religious zeal justified verbal and physical assaults, and Christian emperors threatened non-Christians with loss of property and exile and even death. But Gibbon and many others may have overstated the importance of religion in late antiquity; partly because of their own views, but also because Christian writings dominate the textual record and give prominence to church councils and theological debates and elections of bishops, as if these were at the top of a busy emperor's agenda. Histories and chronicles, sermons and theological treatises, reports of church councils and the lives of saints and martyrs survived because Christian readers cared about them, and because monastic communities had the resources of labour and materials to make copies.

Texts also survive from other religious traditions, but they are not as varied as the Christian texts, and it is much more difficult to give them a specific context in time and place. Jewish scholars in the Roman and the Persian empires compiled the Talmud, which survives in two versions from Jerusalem and Babylon. Its present form may be as late as the 6th century, and it reports perhaps three centuries of discussion on Jewish law and scripture. Early Islamic tradition, from the 7th and 8th centuries, is also complex and difficult to date, and scholars debate how the Qur'an was formed. These three traditions are known as 'religions of the book' because of their central sacred texts, but late antiquity was

5. A page of the *Codex Sinaiticus*, a complete Greek text of the Bible

bookish, and other texts were also regarded as a source of wisdom. Philosophers used commentary on Plato's writings as a way of developing their own interpretations of God and the universe, asking how best the immortal soul can return from this messy material existence to its true home with God. Some also saw true wisdom hidden in Greek texts which they believed to be the product of traditions even more ancient than their own, such as the Hermetic Corpus ascribed to Egypt and the Chaldaean Oracles ascribed to Babylon.

All these texts may come from a small minority whose powerful writings have survived. It does not follow that all or most people shared their perspective, especially when education was expensive and even basic literacy, on one estimate, may have been as low as 10%. But provided that one person in a group could read, others could listen, and books are not the only way to learn. Christian churches offered teaching of a kind which was not provided at the temples of Greek and Roman gods, or accessible in the lectures and seminars of philosophers. Their sacred texts were available in bookshops, or even in free copies, and explanation was free to anyone who came to church. Preaching, daily or weekly, also offered moral instruction and ways to deal with disaster: barbarian invasions are punishment for sin, famine requires Christian charity, and both are a wake-up call for survivors. But we do not know how many people heard such preaching, and how many of those who heard were also moved to act.

Churches and donors offered practical and emotional support for people who wanted to commit their lives to prayer and study. This opened up new choices, especially for women. Women were expected to marry, keep house, and have children, unless their social and economic situation forced them to do otherwise. Men too were expected to marry. Philosophers taught their students that the wise man owed his parents grandchildren, his city new citizens, and the gods a new generation of worshippers; marriage might seem to be a distraction from philosophy, but the responsibilities of a household offered training in the 'political' virtues of engagement with other people. Sexual desire was not a prominent theme in these lectures, because it was assumed that the wise man would control all his desires, and would be faithful to his wife as she was to him. But some Christians argued for life virginity, or failing that, celibacy, for women and men, as the physical analogue of commitment to God, and as liberation from the compulsions of desire. Augustine was careful not to devalue marriage (after all, God invented it), but saw it as a second best. He thought that households were built from dominance relationships: husband and wife, parents and children, master and slave. Monasticism offered instead life in a community of brothers or sisters.

The Greek word *monachos,* 'monk', comes from *monos,* which can mean 'alone' in the sense 'solitary'. *Monos* can also mean 'single' in the sense 'integrated', in contrast with multiplicity and distraction. Some ascetics did attempt a solitary life, but experience showed that communities provided structure and guidance, practice in loving your neighbour, and more effective help for the poor. Basil of Caesarea observed that a monk should not give his only garment to someone in need, but should find the brother in charge of the clothing store. Gibbon, reading the complaints of pagan texts about black-robed consumers, may have underestimated the work monks did to support themselves and to help the poor. In Egypt, in the time of Constantine, Pachomius established pioneering monastic communities which were successful farming collectives, producing a surplus for the poor because their members were not responsible for families. Monks who followed the example of Antony and retreated into the desert, that is, the uncultivated land, could prepare and plait rushes as a technique of resistance to distraction, and make baskets to sell for subsistence and for the poor. Gibbon may have also accepted too readily the claims of Christian texts that thousands renounced the world of work and family. Augustine, at Milan in the late 4th century, was not aware that Ambrose had established a community of 'good brothers' outside the city walls. In 6th-century Egypt and Syria, there were large monastic buildings on the outskirts of villages, but they still held only a small proportion of the local population.

Religious intolerance too can be overestimated. Fierce polemic and strongly worded laws survive as texts, but most people, most of the time, lived at peace with their neighbours, no matter how vehemently their emperors denounced heretics, or how eloquently their bishops tried to keep them from attending local festivals, or from using pagan or Jewish magic when a child was ill. Sermons reveal that congregations had far more flexible views on the Christian life than their bishops wanted. But religion could still be a powerful way of affirming identity, especially in opposition to another identity which might be created, or made more distinct, for the purpose. In times of confrontation, people were classed as pagans, Jews, heretics, and classed themselves as Christian, catholic, orthodox; but all these definitions have been questioned.

Identity and confrontation

Christian martyrs, according to their stories, sometimes responded to a judge's request for name and status by saying only 'I am a Christian': a chosen identity, not an ethnic or civic or ascribed identity. Nobody said 'I am a pagan', because 'pagan' is a disparaging Christian term for non-Christians. The nearest equivalent is 'I have always worshipped the gods', and that could usually be taken for granted. But when the emperor Decius came to power in the civil wars of the mid-3rd century, he ordered all inhabitants of the empire to sacrifice to the gods, not just by attending a festival but by making libations and tasting the meat of the sacrificial victims, and he wanted a certificate to prove it.

Some certificates survived in the hot dry climate of Egypt. Like census records, they identify those who sacrifice by name, physical characteristics, place of residence, or status. They state that the person sacrificing has always worshipped the gods with libations and sacrifices, and now requests the relevant official to certify that he or she has done so again. Some certificates cover several people, presumably the members of a household, and the letters of Cyprian bishop of Carthage show that people who had not in fact sacrificed found ways to get certificates. Even so, it is difficult to imagine how Roman officials could cope with 'all inhabitants of the empire'. Christian authors thought that Christians, who did not sacrifice to any god, were the real target for Decius and for his successor Valerianus, who ordered more specific attacks on Christian clergy. Persecution, they noted, does not pay. Decius was

6. Martyred saint, probably St Laurence, with bookcase

the first Roman emperor to die in battle, and Valerianus was the first to be captured alive: Sapor, king of the Persians, kept him in chains, dressed in imperial purple, and used him as a mounting-block.

At the end of the 3rd century, Diocletian denounced Manichaeans, whose prophet Mani came from Mesopotamia, as a sinister Persian force undermining Roman ancestral virtue. A few years later, perhaps because wars were going badly, he also denounced Christianity. Lactantius, a Christian who taught rhetoric at the imperial court, said that Christian courtiers at Constantinople attended sacrifices in the course of their duties, but made the sign of the cross to protect themselves against demons. For non-Christians, a sign which commemorated a dying man meant that the gods would not reveal their will in the sacrifice, because the immortal gods want nothing to do with mortality. Diocletian ordered the destruction of churches and scriptures, and deprived Christians of rank and status so that they were not protected against torture. This 'Great Persecution', as it was known to

Christians, had different effects in different regions of the empire. The church historian Eusebius reported horrific deaths in his homeland of Palestine, where his own teacher died from the effects of torture. In North Africa, where every detail was remembered in later disputes, there were some executions, but the chief demand was that Christians should hand over their scriptures, and sometimes the authorities accepted other impressive-looking texts. In Britain and Gaul, Constantius, father of Constantine, had some churches pulled down, but apparently did little else.

Constantine's soldiers proclaimed him emperor at York in 306. Six years later, after a victory he ascribed to the God of the Christians, he was able to declare an end to persecution and to proclaim freedom of worship. The balance shifted in the course of the 4th century. Constantius, son of Constantine, claimed to follow his father's precedent when he banned public sacrifice. Julian, known to Christians as 'the Apostate', declared freedom of religion, refused to take part in Christian disputes, and tried to revive the tradition of sacrifice. At the end of the century, Theodosius I banned all manifestations of pagan cult, even the burning of incense before the household gods. But Christian emperors made appointments without insisting on religion, and even in the 6th century, when Justinian excluded pagans, Jews, and heretics from public service, they were not at immediate risk of a cruel public death and there are few examples of actual punishment. Persecution of pagans, like persecution of Christians in the first three centuries, happened at specific times and places because of local crises or because someone saw an opportunity to attack an enemy.

The most horrific example of a pagan death was not authorized by law. Alexandria had a long tradition of conflict among groups who could claim a religious or cultural identity: Jews and Greeks, Christians with different theologies and loyalties, philosophers and their students rushing to defend the temple of

Sarapis when monks and soldiers combined to attack it. Hypatia, who died in 415, was a most unusual woman. She was the daughter of a philosopher, and might have been expected to marry a philosopher and live a principled life. Instead, she did not marry, but taught philosophy and appeared in public in the presence of officials, activities traditionally reserved for men. The Christian historian Socrates, who admired her dignity, said that a Christian mob blamed her for the bad relationship between Orestes, prefect of the city, and the bishop Cyril. They seized her and took her to a church, where they stripped her and scraped off her skin with potsherds and shells. In the 5th century, this death was so shocking that different groups of Christians blamed each other. In the 7th century, the Coptic writer John of Nikiu claimed that Hypatia was a pagan magician inspired by the devil to lure Orestes away from church, that the ringleader in her death had official status, and that she died from being dragged through the city.

Persecution of Christians did not end when there was a Christian emperor, for disagreements about right belief could develop into violent attacks invoking the memory of martyred leaders. Sometimes emperors tried to restore order by imposing agreed statements, requiring an end to discussion, and having books publicly burned; not that any of this ever worked. Emperors intervened in religious disputes because they were inevitably an aspect of politics. Constantine set the precedent soon after he achieved control of the eastern empire: in 325 he summoned bishops to a council at Nicaea, in northern Asia Minor, and offered them a formula to use in an agreed statement on the relationship of Jesus Christ to God the Father. Eusebius, who had lived through persecution, was moved by the experience of attending a council where the emperor asked permission to sit and his troops formed a guard of honour for bishops. He still had difficulty explaining to his congregation why he had accepted the agreed statement and its rejection of opponents: 'let him be anathema', that is, accursed.

Some historians think that Constantine was shocked by the bitter theological disputes he found, and saw it as his responsibility to resolve them, just as his predecessors tried to unite the empire in reverence for the gods. They think he was serious, not ignorant, when he said that theological debates should be left to theologians. He could have compared the debates of philosophers, who, as Augustine pointed out, disagreed about every aspect of life without anyone feeling the need to settle their questions. Other historians think that involvement in theological disputes was the price Constantine had to pay for practical and rhetorical support from Christian bishops, especially for their help in clearing the backlog of lawsuits.

Either way, Constantine set the precedent for imperial intervention which made divisions worse. Some bishops who could not sign up to Nicaea were exiled, and many more Christians could not accept Nicene theology, or simply stayed loyal to their leaders and traditions. They were labelled 'Arians', and they included most Goths, not because Goths had any direct connection with Arius the Alexandrian priest, but because the missionaries who taught them had similar views. Sixty years after Nicaea, while Augustine was in Milan, the Gothic bodyguard of the under-age emperor demanded, with the backing of his powerful mother Justina, a church where Arian services could be held. Bishop Ambrose refused. His congregation, including Augustine's mother Monnica, occupied the disputed church, and as the soldiers arrived with imperial purple hangings, they kept up morale with congregational singing in the style he had learned from friends in the eastern churches. Ambrose won that confrontation, but Goths continued to be Arian. In the post-Roman kingdoms of western Europe, 'Arian' and 'Catholic' became markers of political loyalties, and Gregory, bishop of Tours, claimed that babies might die if the wrong kind of Christian baptized them.

In North Africa, two groups of Christians claimed to be the true catholic (that is, universal) church to which Constantine offered funding. Each group accused the other of betraying the scriptures during the persecution under Diocletian, of invoking the power of the state to deal with religious matters, and of humiliating, maiming, and killing members of the other group. In 411, after a century of conflict, an imperial commissioner was sent to Carthage in a final effort to resolve the dispute. The official record survives to show that each group had maximized its numbers by establishing bishops in every village and farmstead, each exploited all possible legal technicalities, and everyone had bitter memories of conflict. Augustine was very active in opposition to the group who were labelled 'Donatists' (after a leader called Donatus). He said that there was a serious theological difference, for Donatists refused to love their neighbours. They insisted that sinners cannot be part of the church, as if it were Noah's Ark carrying pure and selected creatures over the stormy sea of the world. Augustine thought of it as a net in the sea: we shall not know until the end of time who is within it. In 411, the Donatists lost, but their churches continued. These divisions may have weakened resistance to the invasion of North Africa, twenty years later, by the Vandals, who were Arian.

In the eastern empire, religious divisions had even greater impact. The council of Chalcedon, in 450, was intended to complete the work of Nicaea. It would have met at Nicaea, but the emperor Marcian, who also had to deal with barbarian attacks, asked the bishops to convene nearer Constantinople. Once again, some would not sign the agreed statement of belief. They were labelled 'Monophysites', because they were thought to understand Christ as having a single (*monos*) divine nature (*physis*), rather than two natures, divine and human; it would have been better to understand *monos* as 'single' in the sense 'integrated'. Theological differences were complicated by language. Distinctions which worked in Greek did not work in Syriac, which was widely used in the near east, or in Latin when disputants sought the support of western churches. As at Nicaea, many Christians thought it was a mistake to move from the words of the Bible to the vocabulary of

Greek philosophy, and chose to stay with their traditions and their leaders; the 'monophysite' tradition continues in Eastern Orthodox churches. A century after Chalcedon, Justinian was still trying to find a formula which everyone could accept. When his troops reconquered North Africa from the Vandals, he had to deal with resistance to his religious policy both from Arians and from Catholics. A century after that, in the 640s, the emperor Heraclius also struggled to find a formula as religious divisions weakened resistance to Arab invasions and made some of his subjects see Roman emperors as enemies of the true faith.

Influence

Religion can affirm identity; it can also be a way of achieving and maintaining influence. The members of the social elite who held traditional Roman priesthoods expected to take a leading role in the community, and could pay for sacrifices and festivals, with stage performances and shows and distributions to citizens. When Christian emperors banned sacrifice, festivals were allowed to continue as entertainment, and temples were maintained as heritage:

> Although all superstition must be thoroughly rooted out, we nevertheless wish the temple buildings situated outside the city walls to remain intact and undamaged. Many stage shows, circus games and contests have their origin here, and it is not right to tear down places from which the celebration of traditional pleasures is offered to the Roman people.

Constantius, son of Constantine, issued this law in 342. The general policy continued, but officials sometimes prompted, or disregarded, attacks by local zealots on a temple or a statue. In the 380s, for example, there was an attempt on the temple of Zeus at Apamea in Syria, a centre of traditional religion and philosophical teaching. A military commander decided that the building was just too strong to demolish, but Bishop Marcellus used local labour and had at least some effect. He went on to attack other temples, but the local people defended them, and Marcellus was seized and burned. At Aphrodisias, in Asia Minor, hostility to pagan visual culture was more selective. The city's guardian deity Aphrodite (Venus) was the mother of Aeneas and was claimed as an ancestress by Julius Caesar. In honour of Rome and its emperors, two colonnades led to a temple, and all the façades had rows of relief sculpture commemorating emperors, heroes, and gods. By the mid-7th century, one colonnade was re-used for shops, and the other had collapsed, thus preserving the relief sculpture which had been carefully and selectively defaced. Male and female genitals on nude statues were excised; emperors and the heroes and heroines of legend were untouched; but the surface of gods and goddesses was removed with a pick. Aphrodisias was renamed Stauropolis, 'city of the Cross'.

Even if there were no sacrifices, and no overt cult, some bishops thought that traditional festivals were a threat to morals and to the soul. They did not always convince their congregations, but they tried. Augustine's longest surviving sermon lasted over two hours, until he was sure that the local stage show was safely over. He urged his hearers to be martyr fans, not actor fans. Why, after all, were they passionate about a profession which was legally and socially degraded? Imagine the reaction, he asked them, if you said to a friend: 'You think that actor is really great, don't you? Well, I hope your son will grow up to be just like him!'

Church ceremonies had rival attractions. Well-resourced churches were full of light and colour, with clusters of oil lamps set among reflective silver disks; hangings of precious fabrics embroidered with gold; multicoloured tesserae, faceted to catch the light, in wall and floor mosaics which portrayed saints and donors and Bible stories. Constantine's benefactions to churches in Rome included candelabra, with endowments of farms to maintain the supply of olive oil for the lights. John Chrysostom described the journey of a martyr's relics from Constantinople to a church along

7. Basilica of Santa Costanza, Rome: massive construction but flooded with light

the coast: the empress came too, the city was deserted, and the torches were like a river of fire. On the evidence of reproachful sermons, vigils and martyr-feasts were also time for a party, which could be as riotous as a traditional festival. Paulinus, bishop of Nola, was a Roman aristocrat, one of the few known to have given up property and status for an ascetic life. He carefully explained that when animals were butchered and roasted at a festival, this was not a sacrifice, but an offering in honour of the martyr, to be shared with the poor. Some farmers, he wrote, brought an exceptionally fat pig in honour of St Felix. The pig could not keep up, and they left it by the roadside; but when they reached the shrine they found it waiting.

Churches also offered dramatic readings about the trial and death of martyrs, and emotionally intense preaching. We do not know how many people came and how they felt, because all we have is the words of church leaders. Some, recorded by shorthand writers, refer to lively audience reactions. In one collection of sermons by Augustine, rediscovered in the late 20th century, a congregation refuses to be told off for its behaviour the previous day, and chants *Missa fac! Missa missa fac!*, 'Mass! Mass! Do the Mass!' At its best, preaching was expert rhetoric, and provided free literary and philosophical teaching of a kind which otherwise cost serious money. Anyone could come to church in Hippo to hear Augustine, former professor of rhetoric at the imperial capital Milan. At Caesarea in Cappadocia, they could hear Basil, another professional, who could have worked in higher education or the imperial service. At the other end of the range were the priests in the country districts around Arles, whose sermons were so bad that their bishop Caesarius distributed copies of sermons by Augustine for them to read out instead. But at least there were efforts to reach beyond the cities. In the North African countryside, Punic was the local language, and Augustine tried to find Punic-speaking clergy. In many regions, Christian preaching, translation of scripture, and theological writing used local languages. Gothic and Armenian alphabets were devised for Bible translations, and Coptic, which is Egyptian written in Greek letters, was strongly associated with Christian texts.

A bishop who could preach a powerful sermon, had many people enrolled on his welfare list, and had personal connections with officials and leading families, could exert influence like a politician who could make a powerful speech and had contacts and dependants. He could call on his congregation to increase the welfare fund. He had the judicial authority given him by Constantine, though Augustine said that was a mixed blessing: before the judgement, everyone praised the bishop, but after it, one side blamed him for wanting to please the rich or to look like the champion of the poor. Local governors had to reckon with the bishop's ability to muster religious protests and chanting crowds, sometimes supported by muscular bath attendants or by tough monks ready to die for the cause.

Religion can exploit the power of rhetoric to influence beliefs, behaviour, and willingness to give money or even life; and religion offers stronger incentives than politics. But, on the evidence we have, late antiquity was not full of religious violence, world-renouncing ascetics, influential bishops, and people who identified themselves by their religious beliefs. 'Secular' comes from the Christian contrast of *saeculum,* 'the present age', with the life to come; it was possible to live a secular life, rarely if ever affected by religion.

Chapter 5
What shall we do to be saved?

Religion as an aspect of politics is a modern interpretation. Many of the texts which survive from late antiquity are concerned with religion as the relationship of divinity with humanity. What shall we do to be saved, that is, to save our souls from death or degradation? Greek tradition said 'remember you are mortal', but Platonist philosophy said 'remember you are immortal': that is, remember that you are an immortal rational soul housed in a mortal body. What lifestyle, and which gods, would help this soul return to the company of immortal spiritual beings? Traditional religion honoured the gods with sacrifice, but do gods really want dead animals, or any other offering that humans can give, other than pure thoughts about the gods? Traditional myths did not provide pure thoughts, and Plato argued in *Republic* that poets tell lies about the gods. Homer's gods disagree, have love-affairs with mortals, fight each other in support of their human favourites, and grieve when those favourites die. But a god who is worthy of worship must be one, and wholly good.

Augustine said that Platonist philosophers came closest to the truth about God and the world, but they failed to understand God's gift of Jesus Christ and of the constant help which makes human moral effort possible. Philosophers, he said, also failed in their duty to their fellow citizens. They taught that the gods are not like man-made images and do not want blood sacrifice, yet they took part in sacrifices to images; they did one thing in public and said another to their students in private. But there was an answer to this charge. The ancient traditions of Greek and Roman religion, and the stories and rituals and imagery associated with their gods, could be interpreted as expressions of profound truths shared with other ancient traditions.

8. The philosopher focused on the other world

One widely used solution was to interpret the many gods as aspects, or agents, of the one god, operating at different levels of the universe and in different contexts:

> Greece tells the story, without firm evidence, that Mount Olympus is the dwelling-place of the gods. But we see and prove that the forum of our city is occupied by a gathering of saviour gods. Who is so insane, so deluded, as to deny the utter certainty that there is one highest God, without beginning, without offspring in nature, like a great and glorious father? We invoke under many names his powers that are diffused through the created world, because, obviously, none of us knows his name: God is the name common to all religions. So it is that while we honour his parts (so to speak) separately, with various supplications, we are clearly worshipping him in his entirety.

This is part of a letter from Maximus of Madaura, which survives because he wrote it to Augustine. Maximus was a teacher of literature in the African town where Augustine went to school. He could claim that 'everyone knows' the many gods are aspects of the one god because that was what teachers taught their students as they worked through Virgil or, in Greek-speaking regions, Homer. According to the Christian historian Orosius, these interpretations were so common that when pagans were confronted with Christian arguments, they replied 'we don't worship many gods, we venerate many agents who are subordinate to the one god'.

Plato suggested, in *Symposium*, that there are beings intermediate between gods and humans. Later philosophers developed this suggestion. They thought that the gods live at the highest level of the universe, in the aether, which is immaterial fire. The sun and stars are visible gods, made of material fire. Below aether and fire is air, which becomes denser and damper, like mist, as it descends, until it condenses as water. The lowest level is earth. Human bodies are dense and moist and mortal, but the gods have given us rational minds, so we can reason our way towards understanding the universe, and the more we move from particulars to principles, the closer we are to thinking the thoughts of God. Our souls may rise to immortality among the stars; perhaps they can be seen in the Milky Way. Between us and the gods are the *daimones*. Humans are rational mortal beings, *daimones* are rational and immortal; but gods do not have bodies, whereas *daimones* have bodies of the most tenuous substance. So we cannot see *daimones*, but they can operate at this lowest level of the universe.

Daimones can go either way. Their rational mind should be in control of their tenuous body, so that their thoughts and purposes are not distinct from those of the one god. But if they allow their own desires to take over, they may be harmful to humans. This was a useful explanation for bad things happening, and in the late 3rd century the Platonist philosopher Porphyry of Tyre took it further. His treatise *Abstinence* collects arguments for and against vegetarianism, which he thought was the appropriate way of life for the true philosopher. Modern readers are interested in his discussion of intelligence and emotion in animals and birds, but Porphyry had more to say about blood sacrifice, because it provided an argument that the gods approve the killing and eating of animals. Homer's gods have their own special food and drink, ambrosia and nectar, but they are pleased by the smell which rises from meat roasting at a sacrifice. Porphyry suggested that the gods who require sacrifice are not poetic fictions: they are *daimones* who want to feed their airy bodies on the thick fatty smoke, so they deceive humans into believing they are gods.

Christian authors knew from the Psalms that 'the gods of the nations are demons', and were quite prepared to acknowledge that these gods had real, though limited, power to deceive and harm. They identified the *daimones* with the fallen angels who rebelled against God. Augustine claimed that in his time, *daimon* was always used in the bad sense 'demon', so that not even a philosopher would say to his slave 'you have a *daimon*' and mean it as a compliment. But Augustine had not read the work of Porphyry's later contemporary Iamblichus, who thought that traditional rituals were appropriate offerings to the *daimones* in charge of different aspects of the universe. Augustine expected his readers to be shocked by sexually explicit rites, but Iamblichus argued that even processions of phallic symbols and shouts of obscenities honoured the *daimones* in charge of procreation.

How then could he explain why sex and birth caused religious pollution and were excluded from sacred ground? Iamblichus suggested that these prohibitions also expressed religious truth, by recognizing that the rational soul must descend from its true home among the gods when it joins with a mortal body. But Platonist philosophers did not always interpret this descent as punishment for crimes in a previous life, or as a fall driven by the soul's desire for the body or by its reckless wish to decide for itself. Some, like Iamblichus, thought that the god has sent rational souls to take charge of every level of the universe. The human soul which is joined with a body must remember its origin and work to be worthy of return; reason must control the desires of the body, so that natural needs are met but excessive or unnatural wishes are resisted. Philosophers, that is, lovers of wisdom, should live simply, but it is appropriate for men and for women to marry and have children and to be householders and citizens.

Iamblichus offered his students a version of the philosophic life which could be combined with social duties. He traced it back to the first man to be called a philosopher: Pythagoras, he claimed, founded communities in which households managed their property in common, and the daily routine included meditation and exercise and discussion, yet administrators found time (after lunch) to devise laws for local cities. Porphyry, at least in *Abstinence*, offered a much more austere version for the true philosopher, who tries to minimize the distractions of bodily needs. This philosopher eats the minimum of simple vegetarian food; there is no suggestion that he has a household and a family; in words borrowed from Plato, he cannot tell you the way to the Town Hall, and he is so out of touch with dinner-party gossip that he does not even know what he does not know. But this philosopher, one of a minority even among philosophers, comes nowhere near the extreme austerity of some Christian ascetics.

Christian monastic life is a late antique social revolution. Men and women gave up wealth, status, and family ties to live in single-sex celibate communities, without personal possessions, their lives committed to prayer, Bible study, and care for the poor. This was an entirely new possibility for women. For the first time, it was worth writing the lives of women, because their spiritual efforts were more interesting than their domestic lives. It was also a new possibility for most men. A few philosophers chose not to marry, but the rare examples of religious communities were all located in exotic cultures: Egyptian priests, Jewish Essenes, Indian Brahmans. Some Christian imagery challenged gender expectations as well as social roles: women were praised for manly courage and for making their bodies masculine; men were praised as manly eunuchs who had cut off sexual desire and weakened their male strength by fasting; both could be spiritually pregnant with children for God. Monastic communities were designed as a new way of living for people who confronted their demons and acknowledged their bad thoughts, so that they were free to focus on love of God and love of neighbour. But some Christians presented this way of life as obviously better than faithful and fertile marriage at the centre of a household which was generous in charity; and some praised extreme forms of asceticism which resulted in starvation and isolation, sleep deprivation, and self-harm.

In the 5th century, Simeon the Stylite chose to live for 40 years on the top of a 50-foot pillar (*stylos* in Greek), exposed to heat and cold and rain and wind in the mountain country beyond Antioch, eating and drinking very little, prostrating himself in prayer so often that Theodoret, bishop of Cyrrhus, lost count as he watched, and damaging his spine and stomach as well as his gangrened feet. Why? But people travelled to see him, and his fame spread. Theodoret claimed that every workshop in Rome had a protective image of Simeon on his pillar; a gold plaque from Syria shows the holy man seated above a snake which coils around his pillar and rears up at him. Perhaps Simeon was seen as the front line of resistance to demonic forces, or his choice to endure physical suffering inspired others who had no choice. Or perhaps texts which advocate extreme asceticism are examples of sensational late antique rhetoric, expressing the concerns of a vocal minority, and surviving because they were copied. Some Christians strongly opposed arguments for the ascetic life; most disregarded them. Experiments in asceticism gave way to life in community, with rules of life which forbade harsh individual choices and allowed for differences in physical and spiritual strength. The rules devised by Basil and Augustine and Benedict endured because they work.

Late antiquity valued the physical presence of holiness, in a place or a person. Philosophers travelled beyond the Mediterranean world in search of wisdom, and Christians crossed the empire to see the Holy Land or the holy monks of Egypt. Travellers away from home, *peregrini* in Latin, became 'pilgrims' travelling to a holy destination. Some people did not approve, arguing that pilgrimage was physically and morally dangerous, and unnecessary because God is everywhere. If Jerusalem is holy, asked Gregory bishop of Nyssa, why is it so full of crime? Pilgrimage was also unwelcome to ascetics who had withdrawn from the world and did not like it when the world came to them, especially when their visitors were women.

Relics (Latin *reliquae*, remains) could travel to people, because they were distributed as gifts to friends, but bodily relics were a controversial kind of holy presence. The dead were buried outside

9. St Simeon Stylites and the devil as a snake coiled around his pillar

cities, because cities were dedicated to the gods who did not want contact with mortality. Christians called their burial places cemeteries (Greek *koimeteria*), sleeping places for the dead until the resurrection – that is, until they got up (Latin *resurrexi*, I got up). These burials too were usually outside the city, but sometimes the bones and other relics of saints were moved to shrines and churches. This was problematic, both because the dead were in the city, and because Roman law banned disturbance of dead bodies, except when a permit was needed to move them out of danger or from a temporary to a permanent tomb. Christian emperors reaffirmed that this principle applied to the distribution of relics. Some Christians were convinced that even the smallest fragment of the body of a saint, or a possession, or even dust from the tomb, was charged with the spiritual power of these people who lived in union with God. But to non-Christians, miracles associated with relics looked very like magic involving body parts, which were thought to be especially powerful when their owner had died by violence; and some Christians were not convinced that there is any need for veneration of relics when we can pray directly to God.

Rome, 384

Rome is a special case for several reasons: as a city of ancient pagan tradition, as a Christian city of Peter and Paul and many other martyrs, and as a capital city which was no longer an imperial residence. Even so, Rome in the year 384 helps to show the diversity of late antique religion, and the ways in which social status and personal ties helped people to coexist and to circumvent legal restrictions.

The year 384 saw the death of Vettius Agorius Praetextatus, after a distinguished career and a marriage of 40 years to Fabia Aconia Paulina. The emperor Gratian gave permission for his friend Symmachus, prefect of the city, to commemorate him with a statue in the name of the senate. Praetextatus was also a priest of the Vestal Virgins, who served the goddess Vesta at the temple which was the symbolic hearth of Roman kings. Two years earlier, Gratian had ended the exemption of pagan religious officials from public service, and had taken over the funds which maintained pagan sacrifices and ceremonies, but he had not tried to ban the priesthoods or the Vestals. Ambrose of Milan claimed that Rome

10. Symmachus, orator and official, ascends to heaven

struggled to recruit seven Vestals, whereas Christians had thousands of dedicated virgins.

Coelia Concordia, the chief Vestal Virgin, also commemorated Praetextatus with a statue, although Symmachus objected that it was inappropriate for the Vestals to honour a man. Paulina, in gratitude, commissioned a statue of Coelia Concordia, and another statue base records the career of Praetextatus and presents a poem in which Paulina and Praetextatus praise each other. They expected to meet in the afterlife: both were initiates in many rituals now called 'mystery cults', from Greek *mysterion*, something which is 'kept silent' and revealed only to initiates. As proconsul of Greece, Praetextatus got the all-night ritual of the ancient Eleusinian Mysteries exempted from a general ban on nocturnal sacrifices; he and Paulina were initiates. Paulina was a votary of the Egyptian goddess Isis and of the moon-goddess Hecate, who is often associated with witches, but in late antiquity was understood as a mediator between gods and humans. As an initiate of Cybele, Mother of the Gods, Praetextatus experienced the *taurobolium*: his Christian contemporary Prudentius wrote that the priest of Cybele stands in a trench below a grid on which a bull is sacrificed, and is purified by the rain of blood. Praetextatus also reached the highest grade in the cult of Mithras, the Persian deity who mediated between humans and the sun-god. Nothing suggests that in 384 it was dangerous for a Roman aristocrat to follow these cults instead of the emperor's example.

Perhaps 50 years later, Macrobius wrote a long philosophical dialogue, the *Saturnalia*. Its setting is the house of Praetextatus, where Roman aristocrats gather to spend the midwinter festival of Saturn in civilized conversation. Praetextatus, the leading speaker, explains how the gods who are active in our universe, below the heavens, are aspects of the supreme deity: the sun. He argues that the names and attributes of these gods, their cults and their myths, all show awareness of this solar theology. The speakers in the *Saturnalia* never mention Christianity, perhaps because

Macrobius did not want to know, perhaps because he thought it inappropriate in a philosophical dialogue.

Praetextatus allegedly said to Damasus bishop of Rome, who also died in 384, 'make me bishop of Rome, and I'll be a Christian tomorrow'. This was a joke against Damasus, a notoriously rich and influential bishop, but Praetextatus could have thought in terms of adding a bishopric to his other religious offices. Damasus and Praetextatus went back a long way. The historian Ammianus reported that when Damasus was elected bishop in 366, a fight for control of a basilica left 137 dead, and Praetextatus, then prefect of the city, restored order. Ammianus claimed to be impartial, and succeeded so well that there are still debates about his personal religious views: perhaps, like the emperor Julian whom he served and admired, he thought that people should live up to their beliefs. The election of Damasus prompted Ammianus to contrast frugal provincial bishops who live pure and simple lives with luxury-loving city bishops who receive gifts from ladies. Damasus was called 'the married woman's ear-pick', because he whispered in their ears and cleaned them out. A law of 370, addressed to him personally, is probably a response to his request; it may be a rebuke, or he may have tried to pre-empt the competition. This law banned clergy, former clergy, and 'those who wish to be known as continent', from visiting the houses of widows or female wards, and disallowed any gift or bequest they received from a woman 'with whom they had a private connection on the pretext of religion'.

Damasus used his resources to make Rome a more visibly Christian city, building and restoring Christian shrines and churches and burial places, and composing short commemorative poems which were engraved in beautiful lettering. He started Jerome on a project for a New Latin Bible in a style which would not put off classically educated Romans. This was a real problem. Older Latin versions were translations from Greek, and the Greek Old Testament was itself a translation from Hebrew. Augustine described his own reaction when, as a rhetoric student at Carthage, he was inspired by Cicero's praise of philosophy to investigate the Scriptures he had heard as a child. He found the style very poor in comparison with Cicero, and soon gave up. As a bishop, explaining difficult passages, he observed that it often helped to look up the Greek. But Augustine did not know Hebrew, not even the alphabet, whereas Jerome is one of very few non-Jews known to have studied the language. He started to learn from a Jewish convert, he wrote, as a way of keeping his thoughts under control when he was trying to lead the ascetic life in Syria; he kept up his studies in Rome, and resumed them when he left Rome in a hurry and settled in Bethlehem.

Modern scholars think that Jerome overstated his knowledge of Hebrew. He did not translate all of the Bible, and the Latin version which became known as the Vulgate (Latin *vulgata*), the Bible in Common Use, is the work of several translators over time. But he did engage in serious textual scholarship and interpretation. He gave the impression that Jews wanted to keep their traditions to themselves, so his advisors were at risk: a letter to Damasus describes a Jew in Rome bringing texts from the synagogue and insisting that Jerome must drop everything to copy them, and in Bethlehem his Jewish teacher came at night. Jerome's new translation caused problems, as usually happens when familiar wording is displaced. His version sometimes differed from the Septuagint, the Greek translation from Hebrew which, according to tradition, was made by seventy (Latin *septuaginta*) scholars who worked separately, but miraculously produced identical translations. Augustine gently observed that even if they had conferred, their agreement would still be remarkable.

Augustine regretted that Jerome had gone against the authority of the Septuagint. He told the story of a congregation at Oea (near present-day Tripoli) whose bishop introduced Jerome's new version. They were used to hearing that a gourd grew up to shade

70

the prophet Jonah from the burning sun, but Jerome said the word meant 'ivy', not 'gourd'. It seems a small point, but Greek-speakers in the congregation said the text was wrong, there was general upset, and the bishop had to ask the local Jews to confirm the reading. They found against Jerome. This was embarrassing, because Jews often said that Christians had incorrect versions of the scriptures. Some Christians, on the other hand, said that Jews had conspired to change some things in their own texts, in order to undermine the authority of Christian texts. Augustine was not convinced by the idea of a universal Jewish conspiracy; transcription errors, he said, were much more likely.

384 was Jerome's last year in Rome, before scandal and enemies drove him out. He first came to Rome from Stridon (near the Italian border with the Balkans) to be taught by Donatus, whose Latin grammar became a key text for the Middle Ages. He and his friends went for Sunday walks to the catacombs Damasus restored. He may have tried a civil service career before some years of experimenting with the ascetic life, notably on the estate of a friend in Syria. In later centuries, painters depicted him gaunt and penitent in a rocky desert, but his letters suggest a reasonably comfortable hermitage, where friends visited with supplies of books. Back in Rome, he became an assistant to Damasus, and that is why painters, anachronistically, use a cardinal's red hat as his symbol. Jerome could offer stylish Latin, knowledge of Hebrew, and experience of theological debates and ascetic practice in the eastern churches, and on his account, everything went so well that he was expected to be the next pope. But his outspoken attacks made him many enemies, and his influence over the widowed Roman aristocrat Paula, and her daughters Blesilla and Eustochium, may have been the last straw.

Blesilla, widowed at twenty after seven months of marriage, recovered from a severe attack of fever and adopted a rigorous ascetic lifestyle. Jerome praised the pallor which showed the intensity of her fasting. She died in autumn 384, and people

11. Art conveys theology: gold-glass base of a bowl, with married couple and the hero Herakles

blamed him. He had already written to her teenage sister Eustochium the extraordinary Letter 22. It is intensely erotic, and to a modern reader, it appears to encourage the self-disgust, and the rigorous control of food intake, which are characteristic of anorexia. Jerome tells this adolescent that false virgins experience lustful desires, which destroy virginity even if the body is intact. He uses brutal Old Testament imagery to say that a false virgin is a prostitute, sitting in the dust by the road with her skirt over her head and her legs open. He describes how, in the desert, he was beset by fantasies of dancing girls, and how fasting nearly killed him without removing them. He tells Eustochium to stay in her room, avoid married women, and associate with women who are pale and thin with fasting. Paula, the mother of these young women, arranged guardians for her under-age son and his property, then sailed away to visit, with Jerome, the Holy Land and the monks of Egypt. She spent her fortune in charity and on two single-sex monastic communities in Bethlehem, one led by herself and Eustochium, one by Jerome. She died leaving only debts, but, Jerome assured Eustochium, she had laid up treasure in heaven.

Augustine was also in Rome in 384, but his later correspondence with Jerome does not suggest that they met. As a teacher of literature and rhetoric, he had come in hopes of better students than he had at Carthage, where the 'Wrecking Crew' thought it amusing to disrupt lectures. He was helped by the religious movement to which he then belonged. In 384, Augustine was a Manichaean, a follower of the prophet and teacher Mani, who lived in Mesopotamia in the 3rd century AD and was martyred on the orders of the Persian king. The teachings of Mani spread east and west, adapting to local traditions, so that some surviving texts come from Turfan in China, and some from Egypt. In the Roman empire, Manichaeans adapted to Christianity. They identified Mani with the Paraclete (Greek *parakletos*, 'advocate') who, Jesus told his followers, would come to lead them into all truth. Most Christians thought that Jesus meant the continuing guidance of the Holy Spirit. Manichaeans said that he meant Mani, and that the teachings revealed the true hidden meaning of the Scriptures.

This hidden meaning, according to Augustine, was a complex mythological system in which light battled with darkness, the universe was a device for liberating light, and the human soul is a fragment of light trapped in the body, from which it can escape by a disciplined lifestyle and the help of higher powers. The Manichaean Elect maintained poverty and chastity and avoided the taking of any life, even plant life. Their food had to be prepared by their followers, the Hearers, whose lifestyle was less austere, but who were taught to avoid trapping more souls by procreation. Manichaeans were politically suspect, because their religion came from the territory of Rome's eastern enemy, and because they formed secret cells. They were sometimes targeted by laws, and Augustine's opponents later claimed that he had left Carthage to escape arrest; perhaps Rome was safer because there were influential Manichaeans. Augustine did not find better students, but he did meet Symmachus, who had been asked by his relative Ambrose to find a professor of rhetoric for Milan. Augustine got the job; and Symmachus may have been pleased to send Ambrose a professor who was not an orthodox Christian.

Symmachus and Ambrose clashed in what is now the most famous episode of 384; it is not mentioned by Augustine or Jerome. In his anti-pagan measures of 382, Gratian included an order to remove the Altar of Victory from the senate house in Rome. The history of this altar reveals changing imperial attitudes in the 4th century. Senators used to burn incense, make libations, and take oaths at

12. Art conveys theology: the sacrifice of Isaac, from the sarcophagus of Junius Bassus

the altar. In 357, Constantius II, son of Constantine, visited Rome, and showed proper interest in its splendid buildings and ancient traditions. Constantius banned sacrifice, idol-worship, and the use of temples for pagan rituals, but allowed architectural heritage and popular festivals to remain; so he had the altar removed, but left the statue of Victory. Later, perhaps in Julian's reign, the altar was put back, and nobody commented until Gratian had it removed, leaving the statue. Symmachus led a deputation of senators to protest; Damasus organized a counter-protest of Christian senators who said they would not attend the senate if the altar was restored. Then Gratian was overthrown, leaving his 13-year-old brother to succeed him; Pratextatus was praetorian prefect of Italy; and in summer 384, Symmachus became prefect of the city, and was able to include in his official papers a petition to the emperor for the altar to be restored. He offered a memorable summary of a standard argument:

> We ask for peace for the gods of our fathers, our native gods. It is reasonable for whatever people worship to be thought of as one. We see the same stars, the sky is common to all, the same world surrounds us: what does it matter which kind of wisdom each uses to search for the truth? It is not possible to reach so deep a mystery by just one road.

Ambrose used his influence at the court of Milan to resist the arguments of Symmachus. The altar was not restored, except for a brief period in 392 when the pagan Eugenius seized power; the statue remained, but we do not know what became of it.

Was Victory now harmless heritage, a reminder of Rome's glory with no religious implications, or was she still a pagan goddess, powerful or demonic according to your point of view? These arguments continue, in a modified version because few people now worship the gods of Rome; British neo-pagans prefer traditions they believe to be Celtic. Roman religion has been revalued. Augustine presented it as an incoherent mix of little tiny gods with little tiny remits, and raunchy rituals led by politicians who didn't believe a word of it. He said that he got this from Varro, the acknowledged authority on Roman religion, who wrote his *Divine Matters* in the late 1st century BC in an attempt to preserve traditions which were already vanishing. But Varro was still relevant, because he was cited as an authority to the schoolchildren who read Virgil.

In the early 5th century, Augustine's opponents argued that Rome's gods had made Rome a great empire, whereas Christian refusal to worship the gods had allowed barbarians to sack the Eternal City, and Christian ethics were no way to run an empire. The arguments now take the form: Christianity denounced the traditional religion, in which the political and social elite also led religious cult which expressed their commitment to the community. Traditional cult brought the community together in rituals and festivals. It did not make unreasonable demands or foster conflicts about beliefs, and it could accommodate the deities of peoples who were conquered by Rome. In these ways, it did make the empire grow and flourish. Christianity, in contrast, disrupted families, undermined the accepted structures of authority, and fostered bitter religious disputes. Augustine died with Vandals at the gates of his city, but North Africa might have resisted Vandal invasion if he had not helped to divide its population into supporters of Christian factions. The empire as a whole might have been stronger if Christianity had not persuaded people to abandon their duties to family, city, and empire, and to become an extra burden on a hard-pressed economy.

There are counter-arguments. Christian bishops worked very hard if they did their job properly, arbitrating disputes within the community, administering the welfare fund, and doing pastoral work in a society where government did not take responsibility for welfare. Some forceful Christian writers did indeed urge people to abandon family and civic duties, but others praised faithful marriage and urged Christian officials to stay in their jobs. *City of*

God includes Augustine's influential account of why they should do so. Human beings are naturally social, but the world we live in is flawed by the human urge to dominate, which leads to conflict and distrust at every level of society: household, city, empire. Human peace, like Roman peace, must be imposed, by duly authorized people who do not constantly have to exert power. It is a fragile and imperfect peace, but it is far preferable to the alternative.

Chapter 6
Barbarism

Peace and order required defence against those who attacked the empire. The army was a major charge on the budget; enemy attack destroyed resources directly, and absorbed resources which could have been used for Roman citizens. If the enemy was accommodated and assimilated, rather than confronted, that might destroy resources in another way: perhaps the Roman empire was itself barbarized, losing its classical culture and its traditions of discipline and civic pride. 'Late antique' began in art history, as a category of style like 'late Renaissance'. It was not a neutral term. Late antique art was seen as derivative or declining or both. If sculptors, or poets, worked in the classical style, it was because they had run out of ideas; if they did something different, especially if they enjoyed brilliant colours in art and brilliant images in literature, that showed barbarian fondness for bright things, and incompetent handling of classical form.

Procopius described 'Hunnic' fashions for chariot hooligans in 6th-century Constantinople:

> The partisans changed their hairstyles to something new and quite different from that of other Romans. They left moustache and beard untouched, wanting them to grow as long as possible, like the Persians. Their front hair was cut back to the temples, but at the back it hung down long and loose, like the Massagetai, and that was why

they called this style Hunnic. They all saw fit to dress luxuriously, in clothes too elegant for their status; they got these at other people's expense. Their tunic sleeves were very tight at the wrist, then extremely wide to the shoulder, so when they waved their hands as they shouted or cheered in the theatres and hippodromes, that part floated high. Silly people got the idea that their bodies were so splendid and sturdy as to require this kind of covering, not realising that such thin, transparent clothing showed up poor physique. Their shoulder-capes, trousers and shoes were all judged Hunnic in name and style. At first almost all carried weapons openly at night, and by day had two-edged daggers hidden under their clothes. As night fell they gathered in gangs and robbed the upper classes anywhere in the market-place and in the alleys, taking cloaks and belts and gold pins and anything else from the people they encountered.

Was that what it was to be a barbarian: wear strange outfits, carry weapons, and assault decent citizens?

13. Barbaric art? Marble panel from the Basilica of Junius Bassus, Rome

Barbarians got their name because their language sounded to Greeks like bar-bar-bar (or possibly 'rhubarb rhubarb rhubarb'). Some of these non-Greek 'barbarians' were in fact highly civilized people, and some Greeks thought that the 'barbarian wisdom' of Babylonians and Egyptians and Phoenicians was more ancient and more profound than mere Greek cleverness. This argument was useful to Jews, and later to Christians, when they claimed that 'barbarian' Hebrew scripture was more ancient and more profound than Greek philosophy.

The barbarians who threatened Rome in late antiquity were not civilized. They came, not from the ancient city-based cultures of the Near and Middle East, but from the forests and steppes beyond the Rhine and Danube, where they lived on the move or in temporary settlements. Vandals, Goths, Huns, are still bywords for brutal and ignorant destruction of culture. Some Romans thought that barbarians were not just brutal, they were brutes, like brute beasts: ferocious, bloodstained, irrational, less than human. Romans enjoyed stories of social or rational behaviour in animals, but they still categorized animals as either tame or wild. Domesticated animals lived peacefully with humans, making an implicit trade of their produce for human protection. But wild animals were enemies, and there was no way to make peace when they could not understand a deal or keep an agreement.

> Roman, Dahan, Sarmatian, Vandal, Hun,
> Gaetulian, Garamans, Alaman, Saxon – all
> Walk on one earth, enjoy one sky, one ocean
> That bounds our world. Why, even animals
> Drink from our streams; dew that gives grain to me
> Gives grass to the wild ass; the dirty sow
> Bathes in our river, and the dogs inhale
> Our air, whose gentle breath gives life to beasts.
> But Roman and barbarian stand as far
> Apart as biped does from quadruped.

The Christian poet Prudentius wrote this at the end of the 4th century, when many barbarians were Christian, and many were Roman citizens because they had settled within the Roman empire. His contemporary John Chrysostom designated a church in Constantinople to hold services in Gothic for Christian barbarians who served in the Roman army, and sometimes preached there with an interpreter. Did the Goths appreciate the rhetorical skill of John 'Goldenmouth'? The prophet Isaiah, John told his congregation, said that the wolf and the lamb would feed together, and sure enough, 'today you have seen the most barbarian of all men standing among the Church's sheep'.

Until the early 20th century, it was easy to accept the Roman perspective, and to decide that barbarian onslaughts brought down the empire. 'Roman civilization did not pass peacefully away. It was assassinated', the French historian André Piganiol wrote after the Second World War. But some parts of Europe had once been ruled by these barbarians, as the German name for France makes clear: Frankreich means 'kingdom of the Franks'. Patriotic Europeans might take a more optimistic view, accepting but revaluing the Roman narrative of destruction, and arguing that barbarian vigour revitalized a decrepit Roman empire, just as Christian faith replaced a formal Roman religion.

In the later 20th century, as former colonies achieved independence, post-colonial history began to question the perspective of European colonial powers. These powers had claimed credit for bringing savage peoples the blessings of civilization, just as Rome, in the words of Virgil, claimed a divine mission to 'rule the peoples, spare the subject, and fight down the proud'. Post-colonial historians today have the advantage of coming from, or talking to, people who have experienced colonial rule. But when historians of late antiquity began to question the Roman account of barbarians, they faced a problem which often occurs in ancient history: we do not have the other point of view. We do not know what the barbarians thought about it, or how they saw themselves.

'Barbarian' is a Roman category in the same way that 'pagan' is a Christian category. It can be avoided by using specific names, such as Alani or Tervingi or Greuthungi, but these names too come from Roman sources. Modern historians, like late antique Romans, find it difficult to decide just which barbarians they are dealing with. They have the resources of archaeology and linguistic analysis, but late antique barbarians left no verbal record of what they thought and little trace of how they lived, and Roman ethnographers used standard modes of description which do not give confidence that they had seen for themselves. Thus Ammianus, writing in the late 4th century AD about the strange customs of the Huns, has much in common with Herodotus, writing in the late 5th century BC about the strange customs of the Scythians, and shows no wish to understand their culture.

The Huns are little known in ancient records. They live beyond the Mareotic marshes [the Sea of Azov] near the frozen ocean, and they surpass every degree of savagery. From birth the cheeks of children are deeply scored with iron, so that the natural growth of the beard is stunted by the wrinkled scars, and they grow old beardless and without charm, like eunuchs. They are frightening: their limbs are compact and strong, their necks thick, their shape monstrous, so that you would think they were two-legged animals, or like the rough-hewn stumps which are used for the sides of bridges.

Huns, according to Ammianus, live on roots of wild plants and on half-raw meat, which they put under their thighs as they ride, to warm it. They practically live on horseback, buying and selling, eating and sleeping, and conferring. They are used to cold, hunger, and thirst. They feel unsafe under a roof, so they do not have indoor and outdoor clothing. They wear linen, or animal skins; once they put on a tunic, they do not take it off until it falls to bits; they do not have proper shoes.

How can we challenge such descriptions? Gothic is a written language, thanks to the missionary Wulfila, a descendant (according to tradition) of Roman citizens who were taken captive in the 3rd century. He devised an alphabet so that he could translate the Bible for the Goths; he left out the book of Kings, which is full of wars, because Goths did not need any further encouragement to fight. About half of the New Testament translation survives, but very little of the Old Testament. No other Gothic literature survives, nor does any literature in the languages of Huns and Vandals, and linguists think that these languages had little impact on the development from Latin to Romance. Material culture too is in short supply. Some beautifully made weapons and ornaments have survived, but it is difficult to give them a context, because these high-quality items are likely to have been given or traded. There is some archaeological evidence for settlements, but the settlements show a mix of cultural influences, not distinct cultures. All we can conclude is that barbarians did not keep to ethnic groups with distinct origins and names and languages and lifestyles, and that they did form shifting confederations, just as Roman historians and politicians complained. So historians who want to avoid the term 'barbarians' call them 'Germanic peoples', that is, peoples who came from the huge geographical area called Germania, which included Scandinavia and stretched from the Rhine and Elbe eastward to the Danube and Vistula.

Adrianople, 378: barbarians defeat an emperor

Around 375, a confederation of Germanic warrior groups moved from the steppes into regions north of the Danube. Romans called some of them Huns, and archaeologists and linguists debate whether some of these Huns descended from the Hsiung-nu of central Asia, who appear in Chinese sources as a dominant power in the 3rd century. Regime change in the mid-4th century displaced the Hsiung-nu from northern China to threaten the northern territory of the Sassanian empire in Persia, and this was the time when the Gothic peoples north of Ukraine moved south into Roman territory. Goths had done this before, but not on the same scale. Throughout the 4th century, Romans and Goths alternated periods of confrontation with periods of better relations when Goths settled on Roman land and served in the Roman army, Roman officials made diplomatic gifts to Gothic kings, and border regions were open to trade. But the Gothic migration of the late 370s was not successfully handled. The result was a major battle in 378 at Adrianople (Hadrianopolis, 'city of Hadrian', now Edirne), on the route leading west from Constantinople. Roman discipline was supposed to prevail against crude barbarian strength, but in 378 the Roman army lost, the emperor Valens was killed, and according to Ammianus, so were two-thirds of his troops. Did Adrianople result from specific mistakes in diplomacy and tactics, or was it a first sign that Roman manpower could not cope?

Barbarians were warriors, who sometimes farmed, and sometimes took supplies by raiding or threats. Rome's ancient tradition of citizen soldiers had long since been replaced by a professional army. Pay, food, and supplies for the troops took a large share of revenue, perhaps one third of the budget, but army pay was chronically late and inadequate. Where possible, it was supplemented by loot, handouts from commanders, and requisitioned labour and supplies. But nobody could predict where the next threat would come and what resources would be available to meet it, so it was hard to decide how much territory the Romans should try to defend. Natural boundaries, like the Rhine and the Danube and the Euphrates, did not always match political or military boundaries. In some areas, frontiers were marked by major works, like the walls and milecastles and ditches of Hadrian's Wall, or the roads and fortresses in the Negeb and the Sahara. But a frontier can be interpreted in many ways: as a defensible border, or a statement of intent, or a demarcation line, or a zone of interchange.

Roman commanders tried everything: standing armies, mobile armies, rapid-response forces, veterans settled as a territorial army to spread Roman culture. Barbarians too could be hired to serve in the Roman army, or allowed to settle in frontier land which they would defend against the next invaders. Barbarians were not united, even against Rome as the common enemy. In Milan and Constantinople, in the late 4th century, Gothic troops were impressively tall and loyal bodyguards at the palaces of Roman emperors. Stilicho, commander in chief to Theodosius I, was the son of a Roman mother, and of a Vandal father who had served in the Roman cavalry under the same Valens who was killed fighting Goths at Adrianople. Stilicho was, in effect, a half-barbarian emperor. He was linked by marriage with the imperial family, acted as regent in the west, when Theodosius died, for his under-age son Honorius, and claimed also to be regent in the east for his other son, Arcadius. Like his Roman predecessors, Stilicho had to deal with rivals and invasions, and tried negotiation, and buying them off, and fighting. In 406, a Gothic king was defeated in Italy, but a coalition of Vandals, Alani, and Suevi crossed the Rhine into Roman territory. Stilicho was dead, executed on suspicion of treason, before more Goths, led by Alaric, sacked the city of Rome.

Rome, 410: the Gothic sack

The sack of Rome was traumatic. The city was no longer the centre of empire, but it was still a symbol of empire, and its great families still had wealth and prestige. It was also a Christian capital, full of churches and martyr-shrines and religious communities. In Bethlehem, Jerome heard the news in letters from friends. He thought of Virgil's lines on the fire and slaughter which raged as Troy fell to the Greeks, and of biblical laments for Jerusalem left desolate when her people were taken captive to Babylon. He was so distraught, he wrote, that he could scarcely remember his own name, let alone finish his commentary on the prophet Ezekiel. In the prologue to that commentary, he said that the brightest light in the whole world was put out; the Roman empire was beheaded; the whole world perished in one city.

Christian readers knew Psalm 79 on the fall of Jerusalem to the Babylonians:

> The heathen have come into God's inheritance and polluted his sanctuary; they have made Jerusalem waste ground; they have made the corpses of God's servants into food for birds, and the flesh of God's holy ones into food for beasts. Their blood was poured out like water around Jerusalem, and there was no one to bury them.

Everyone with a little education knew Virgil on the sack of Troy:

> The ancient city falls that ruled for many years.
> Throughout the streets the lifeless bodies lie
> And in the homes: death's shapes are everywhere.

This extreme version of the sack of Rome was the product of Jerome's personal anguish, and of late antique education, which taught clever boys to respond intensely to literature and to write with rhetorical brilliance. It has convinced many readers, and until recently it was difficult to challenge from the archaeological record. Excavation in the built-up centre of Rome is not easy: how much did the barbarians destroy, and was Rome before the invasion a thriving capital, or a place of crumbling heritage, where, as Jerome asserted, the gilded Capitol was in disrepair and the temples were covered with spiders' webs? There are some inscriptions recording the restoration of public buildings, but perhaps the elite preferred to invest in churches, or in their own great houses, if they had any money to spare after buying off Goths.

In North Africa, much closer to events in Italy, Augustine tried to comfort his congregation. 'Terrible things have been reported to us: slaughter, arson, looting, murder, torture. It is true: we have heard many reports and grieved at them all, we have often wept and could hardly be comforted.' But Augustine's message was that the sack of Rome should be kept in perspective. Roman refugees blamed it on 'Christian times' in which the gods of Rome were neglected.

Augustine pointed out, correctly, that the city was still standing, not wiped off the map like Sodom and Gomorrah; the awful events had lasted for just three days; and Rome had suffered far worse in the times when her gods were worshipped, especially in civil war. He claimed that the barbarians, savage and bloodstained as they were, respected Christian churches as places of sanctuary. Like Jerome, he thought of Virgil's lines on the fall of Troy, but he used Virgil differently, to contrast the Greeks who slaughtered Priam king of Troy at his own household altar with the Goths who escorted Romans to safety in the churches. When, Augustine asked, had Roman troops ever respected temples, and when, in Troy or in Rome, had the gods of Rome ever protected their worshippers?

Some pagans argued that Rome was invaded because its gods were offended by Christian neglect. Some Christians argued that Rome was invaded because it was still too pagan. On the human level, Alaric could enter Rome because he had enough soldiers to blockade the grain ships at the coast, and because the emperor Honorius stayed in Ravenna and did not intervene. Honorius, it was said, had a favourite fighting-cock called Rome, and when a messenger rushed in to cry 'Rome is perishing!' he was greatly relieved to learn that it was the city, not the fighting-cock. To be fair, Honorius had too few troops to confront Alaric, his imperial colleague in Constantinople was not prepared to help, and he could hope that once again the barbarians could be bought off, if he could find out what they wanted or would accept.

What exactly did the barbarians want? Alaric did not attempt to hold the city of Rome, and perhaps had planned only to threaten it. In the two years of negotiations which preceded the invasion, he had asked at different times for status as a Roman commander, for land where his people could settle, for a guaranteed corn supply, and for gold. The historian Zosimus said that he got 5,000 pounds of gold and 30,000 of silver, 4,000 silk robes, 3,000 scarlet-dyed fleeces, and 3,000 pounds of pepper; the luxury goods were of course saleable. Alaric's successor Athaulf supported a rival claimant for Roman imperial power, then changed sides and married Galla Placidia, daughter of Theodosius I, who had been taken prisoner in 410. The Spanish priest Orosius explained this change of mind in his *History against the Pagans*, a detailed demonstration of Augustine's point that Roman history had been far worse before 'Christian times'. Orosius was an optimist about barbarians, especially if they were Christian; he had met some in Spain who, for a small fee, acted as bodyguards and porters for people escaping from other barbarians. He heard a story that Athaulf at first wanted to make the Roman empire into Gothia, the Gothic empire; then, realizing that the Goths were too barbaric to obey laws, he decided to use Gothic power to restore the Roman empire.

Barbarian kingdoms

Events proved that barbarians could obey laws and form states. From the 5th century onwards, some of their coalitions became kingdoms, with law codes which included elements of Roman law. These kingdoms developed a collective identity: Visigoths (West Goths) in southern France and Spain, Ostrogoths (East Goths) in Italy, Vandals in southern Spain and northern Africa, and in later years Franks in France and Lombards in Lombardy. Historians devised histories for them as if they had always been a recognizable people. Jordanes said in his *History of the Goths* that the Goths were the Getae known to Herodotus a millennium earlier; Gregory of Tours began his *History of the Franks* with Adam and Eve, discussed the Christian bishops and martyrs of France, and moved swiftly on to the arrival of the Franks. This process of 'ethnogenesis', finding the origin and history of a people, is of great interest to Europeans, who over the last century have seen so many claims to ethnic unity based on history and language and religion, and on opposition to other groups.

Nobody wrote a history for Attila the Hun, who in the early 5th century dominated a critical mass of warriors based in the

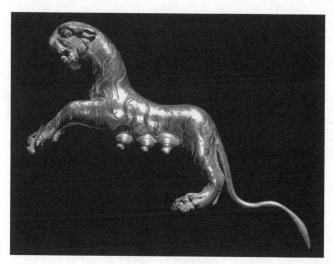

14. **Barbarian art: handle of a silver vessel, from a hoard found in Suffolk**

Hungarian plain. But Jordanes included in the *History of the Goths* a detailed account by Priscus of Panium, diplomat and historian, of his visit to Attila in 448 on an embassy from Constantinople. Priscus called Attila's people Scythians, the ancient name for the inhabitants of South Russia, who appear in classical texts either as barbarians with strange customs or as noble savages uncorrupted by civilization. He met people who spoke some Latin as well as their native Hunnic or Gothic, and he found colleagues from the western imperial court: an Italian sent to be a secretary to Attila, and an embassy trying to resolve a dispute about silver vessels. Greek, he noted, was rarely heard, and most Greek-speakers were captives from northern Greece and the Adriatic. But one Greek merchant, captured in a town on the Danube, had won his freedom by fighting bravely, and was prosperous enough to think Attila's kingdom a great improvement on the corrupt Roman empire. Priscus, of course, disagreed.

Attila did not rule a 'Hunnic empire': his confederation had no lasting structures and laws and did not survive his death. It successfully extorted payment by threat, sometimes with demonstrations of force, but not with invasions, for there was no point in destroying the communities which produced and traded goods for the Huns to take. Priscus the diplomat showed that even in dealing with barbarians, there were ways to acknowledge status, avoid offence, make appropriate gifts, and find people who could help to negotiate. But diplomacy sometimes failed. A year after this embassy, the Roman general Aetius made an agreement with Attila; two years after that, in alliance with Visigoths, he fought off Attila's invasion of Gaul; in 455 the Vandals sacked Rome. Aetius, as a teenager, had been a hostage with the Huns; as a young man he led a force of Huns into Italy in support of a would-be emperor; and in the shifting alliances of Romans and barbarians, he fought both with and against Visigoths.

In the later 20th century, most historians followed Priscus in preferring accommodation to confrontation. This 'Eurobarbarian' model was influenced by the experience and hopes of multicultural European and American cities, where members of different ethnic groups usually lived at peace, developed social relationships, and sometimes intermarried. There is evidence that barbarians were accepted into Roman society, as settlers and soldiers who set up house with Romans. Comparative anthropology showed that nomadic peoples do not move at random: they make informed use of marginal land, so that they can raise crops and livestock at the right time. But in recent years, barbaric barbarians have made a comeback. There is also evidence for violent confrontation, for barbarians as a constant drain on resources of money and manpower, and for a much reduced quality of life in regions taken over by barbarians. It was not a matter of substituting a barbarian king and his leading warriors for a Roman governor and his officials, and leaving law and religion and culture almost unchanged. But some Roman officials did their best to make it seem so.

Chapter 7
Bronze elephants: classical and Christian culture

We learn from your paper that on the Sacred Way, which
antiquity dedicated to many false religions, bronze elephants
are unstable in every way and close to collapse. In the flesh they
live for thousands of years, yet it seems that in their bronze
images the end is near. Let your care restore their proper
longevity by mending their gaping limbs with iron rivets, and
strengthen their declining belly with a supporting wall, lest
that amazing size should be shamefully dispersed in ruin. A
fall is dangerous even for live elephants. When they set their
huge limbs, in a kind of lying down, to trees which have been
felled by human skill, if once they collapse they are prostrated
by their full weight and cannot get up by their own efforts,
because their feet are not made flexible by any joints, but are
permanently rigid and unbending like columns. […] When
this immense animal is restored to its feet, it remembers the
kindness done to it, and takes as its master the one it recognises
as having come to its aid.

This is part of a letter to the urban prefect of Rome from
Theodahad, king of the Ostrogoths, who in the early 6th century
ruled Italy from Ravenna. Why, in dangerous times, was he
interested in bronze elephants? Theodahad was a recent and
insecure ruler. He was first the colleague, then the murderer, of his
cousin Amalasuntha, who became queen regent for her son when

her father Theoderic died in 526. Theoderic the Ostrogoth, the man with a moustache (worth mentioning because Latin has no word for one), was sole ruler of Italy for thirty years, from the early 490s. According to Marcellinus, a loyal follower of Justinian, the last Roman emperor in the west was deposed in 476: he had the splendid name Romulus Augustulus, which combines Romulus, the legendary founder of Rome, with a diminutive of Augustus, the title of Rome's first emperor and of all subsequent emperors. But 476 was not necessarily the end of Roman rule in the west, for there were still potential emperors, there were wealthy and well-connected senators in Rome, there was a Roman emperor at Constantinople who might be convinced to intervene, and there were debates about religion which might give him a reason to do so.

The city of Rome was no longer the centre of the political world, but the bishop of Rome claimed primacy over (at least) the western churches as the successor of the apostle Peter. Bishops of this status were always involved with politics, and Roman senators were involved with church politics and with negotiations on theology between the Roman clergy and the emperor in Constantinople. Theoderic tried to stay on good terms. He visited Rome, went as a pilgrim to St Peter's, met the Senate, contributed to rebuilding the walls and other monuments, and provided bread and circuses for the people. His official correspondence includes a letter to the senator Boethius, praising his ability to translate Greek technical works into Latin, and asking him to commission a sundial and a water-clock as presents for Gundobad king of the Burgundians.

But towards the end of his reign, Theoderic claimed that some negotiations with Constantinople amounted to treason. He accused the senator Albinus; Boethius protested that if Albinus was guilty, so was the entire senate; then Theoderic arrested Boethius, and his father-in-law Symmachus, and condemned both to death. Boethius wrote his *Consolation of Philosophy* in prison, and it became one of the most influential texts of the Middle Ages. It also presents a problem, for other works show that Boethius was Christian, yet this book written in the shadow of death uses the language of philosophy, not of the Bible. Did Boethius turn to philosophy because in time of crisis it mattered most for him, or was he writing for educated Christians who understood what he could and could not say in a philosophical work?

Theoderic killed senators and was accused of killing a pope. He sent Pope John on an embassy to Constantinople, and on his return detained him at Ravenna; John died in custody and was honoured as a martyr. So Amalasuntha inherited a very difficult situation. Procopius wrote that she spoke Gothic, Latin, and Greek, and showed an almost masculine ability to rule; this sounds patronizing, but is high praise compared to what he wrote about other royal women, especially the empress Theodora. Amalasuntha needed all her ability and linguistic skill to negotiate with the new emperor Justinian and with the various power-groups in Italy and the west. When her son died, she took Theodahad as co-ruler, hoping to calm Gothic anxieties that their tradition was giving way to Roman culture. But he had her killed, and this gave Justinian cause to attack the Ostrogoths, as part of his grand plan to reunite the Roman empire. In 535, Justinian sent his general Belisarius to Italy; in 536 Belisarius was welcomed to Rome; and Theodahad, soon after sending the letter about elephants, was killed by a rival.

It seems unlikely that the prefect's paper gave the elephants a high profile. The city of Rome had suffered much more serious damage, bronze elephants were not a cherished ancient monument, and the Sacred Way was sacred to false gods. So perhaps there is a coded message in the long account of live elephants and their relationships with people. The elephant cannot get up unaided, so it is grateful to the man who helps it, and recognizes him as master. The letter presented Theodahad as a civilized barbarian, who, like Theoderic, was interested in Rome; it also reminded the

Roman elite that their great and long-lived city could not get up unaided, and should be grateful to its master.

Cassiodorus: Gothic, classical, and Christian culture

Theodahad did not write this piece of complex Latin. Its author, Cassiodorus, was a Roman aristocrat, who was also a senior civil servant of the Ostrogoth regime. His grandfather was a Roman civil servant, and his father served Theoderic. Cassiodorus knew of one Roman so convinced the future was Gothic that he learned the language and had his sons educated in it, but this, he thought, was a step too far: Roman culture and administration could continue, in Latin, under Gothic kings.

In the service of the Goths, Cassiodorus reached the impressive status of praetorian prefect of Italy, responsible for army supplies, food supplies, and much jurisdiction. He drafted official documents for Theoderic and his successors, and he wrote a *Chronicle* which maximized Gothic contributions to history and minimized conflicts with Rome. He put together twelve books of his letters, form letters, and edicts, including the letter to Boethius about the clocks, because, he said, his friends insisted: they said that the collection would be a tactful training in eloquence for future civil servants who were less well educated.

In Constantinople, John the Lydian also complained that the new civil service intake was ignorant of bureaucratic style, customs, and traditions. His native language was Greek, but he disapproved of the change from Latin as the language of administration; he retired to be a professor, writing on Roman antiquities and Latin etymology. It is misleading to speak of 'the university of Constantinople', because there were no degree programmes or qualifications; but in the 5th century Constantinople had thirteen funded teachers of Latin grammar and rhetoric, fifteen of Greek, one professor of philosophy and two of law, with newly improved lecture rooms which were not available to private teachers.

Cassiodorus, servant of Gothic rulers from 506 to 538, held offices with Roman titles and administered Roman law. His studied Latin style affirmed that bureaucracy and diplomacy, law and literature, continued to flourish under Gothic rule. His eloquence must have worked at the time, unlikely as it seems now:

> Public expenditure fluctuates with the varying nature of the seasons, but can be kept in check if sound instructions accord with local productivity. For where the harvest has been more abundant, procurement is easy, but if there is a requirement for that which hungry barrenness has denied, then the province is harmed, and the desired result will not be obtained.

Well, yes, Minister; but, as with the bronze elephants, there is a point in this elaborate statement of the obvious. This is the start of an official letter noting that Istria has had a good harvest of wine, corn, and oil, so Cassiodorus proposes to substitute payments in kind for some money taxes, and to make compulsory purchases at a price to be decided. This probably unwelcome message is wrapped up in praise of Istria's fertility and the charm of its Adriatic coast. It was more tactful than a brusque instruction, and the fellow civil servant who received it could read between the lines.

Cassiodorus, who bridged the gap between Gothic rulers and Roman bureaucrats, also combined classical and biblical culture. His form letter for the appointment of a Praetorian Prefect begins by tracing this Roman office back to Joseph, who, according to the book of Genesis, was chosen by the Pharaoh of Egypt to manage the corn supply in good years and bad. Cassiodorus worked with Agapetus, bishop of Rome, to establish funded posts for teachers who would expound the Christian scriptures rather than classical texts. This plan was inspired by memories of a Christian school at Alexandria and by reports of a Christian academy at Nisibis in Persia; it failed because Justinian's reconquest left a funding crisis in Italy. But there is a record of an inscription, from a library on the Caelian Hill in Rome, which described the pictures above the bookcases. Agapetus, founder of the library, sat in the long row of 'saints who expounded the divine law', that is, the scriptures.

Justinian's campaign ended the official career of Cassiodorus. We do not know what happened to him when Belisarius took the Gothic capital Ravenna, but a decade later he was in Constantinople, perhaps engaged in diplomacy as an expert on Gothic affairs, certainly engaged in theological discussions. He wrote Latin commentaries on the Psalms, as Augustine had done, but with more display of classical education:

> 'O God, I have hoped in you: Lord, let me not be thrown into confusion for ever.' Here again the lovely face of the hypothetical syllogism smiles upon us, thus:
>
> If, O God, I have hoped in you, let me not be thrown into confusion for ever.
>
> Now, O God, I have hoped in you.
>
> Therefore I shall not be thrown into confusion for ever.

At last Cassiodorus returned to Italy, perhaps in 554 when Justinian decided, too soon, that Italy was at peace and exiles could reclaim their property. Following Roman tradition, Cassiodorus retired to his family estate in Calabria to lead a life of cultivated leisure, and here too he combined classical and Christian culture. He may again have followed the example of Augustine, who on his return from Italy, before he became a priest and bishop, lived in a small community on his modest family property. At the Vivarian (named for its fishponds, *vivaria*), Cassiodorus collected books, commissioned translations from Greek into Latin, trained a staff of copyists, and wrote several books himself. The most famous of these is the *Institutes*, his 'instructions for reading sacred and secular texts'.

The *Institutes* have the standard Latin name for an introductory textbook. They are like an annotated library catalogue, with one book for the Christian scriptures and one for the liberal arts: that is, the skills (*artes*) suitable for a free (*liber*) person who was not a slave and did not have to take orders from someone who paid for his technical skills. Liberal Arts colleges in the United States, and Faculties of Arts in British universities, keep this ancient tradition. Cassiodorus recognized seven liberal arts. First came three concerned with the use of language: grammar, that is, correct and stylish composition; rhetoric, or effective public speaking; and dialectic, the techniques of definition and argument. These formed the *trivium*, the 'three ways' of medieval education. ('Trivial' meaning 'unimportant' also comes from *trivium*, but in the literal sense: where three ways meet at a crossroads, people stop to exchange gossip.) Then came four arts, the *quadrivium*, concerned with basic principles: arithmetic, geometry, music, astronomy. Music, in this context, meant theory not practice. Playing an instrument was a technical skill, but music was audible mathematics.

To anyone who has recently taught in higher education, Cassiodorus seems very familiar. Important texts have gone missing from the library and cannot be replaced, so one has to think of alternatives. Students want reading-lists with clear indications of content and usefulness and level of difficulty. They like summaries, and they are much more likely to do the reading if it consists of relevant excerpts in a single volume, easy to locate, with a pleasing cover and a contents list. Marginal signs can be used to mark, for example, a definition or an idiom, or to show that one passage is relevant to grammar and another to astronomy. Students are limited to resources in their own language, or in translation, because almost no one has competent Greek. Spelling gets worse all the time, partly because pronunciation changes. At the age of 92, Cassiodorus wrote a basic textbook *On Orthography*, because he saw no point in copying texts so inaccurately that readers could not understand them.

Did Cassiodorus save classical culture for the Middle Ages, by safeguarding and copying texts in an out-of-the-way community while wars continued in Italy? It would be good to think so, but we cannot show that Vivarian texts survived for transmission to other libraries. In the late 7th century, Ceolfrith, abbot of Jarrow in Northumbria, visited Rome and brought back a complete Latin Bible: it would be very good to think that a Vivarian text was the model for the 8th-century Codex Amiatinus, made at Jarrow, and now the oldest text of the complete Latin Bible. We cannot be sure. But we can be sure that although his plan with Agapetus failed, Cassiodorus helped to establish education of the kind Augustine envisaged in *Christian Teaching*, a work Cassiodorus very much admired.

Christians and classics

Augustine wrote *Christian Teaching* a century and a half before Cassiodorus returned to Italy. Much of it is about interpreting scripture and preaching its message effectively, but Augustine also asked how far classical culture could be useful to Christian scripture-based culture. He used the Bible story of the exodus from Egypt, when the people of Israel took gold and silver and precious fabrics from their Egyptian neighbours, then reused them in the service of the true God. Egypt, Augustine said, stood for the worldly concerns which Christians must leave behind, but they could take real treasure with them. Classical culture offered moral precepts, truths about the one God, useful institutions, and arts which could be put to good use, provided people remembered what they were for and did not become too concerned with the arts themselves.

In his *Confessions*, Augustine thought that his own classical education had offered false values: omitting 'h' in 'homicide' seemed worse than committing homicide; children absorbed stories of lust and violence; parents, whatever they said, wanted worldly success. But it did not follow that Christians must reject the culture of the world in which they lived. In his early career, Augustine himself taught grammar and rhetoric, the arts which trained young men for public careers. He judged his earlier self harshly, but at least, he said, he tried to live a decent life, and taught his students that they might sometimes defend the guilty, but must never try to have the innocent condemned. In *Christian Teaching*, he claimed that people did not need an expensive education: they could learn rhetorical technique just by listening to the Bible. But he also pointed out that rhetoric could be used in the service of truth, and that people who prefer a plain style should not dismiss truth just because it was presented in high rhetorical style.

Other people were much more confrontational about classical and Christian culture. When Augustine was a child, the new emperor Julian was asked if he wanted to choose the teachers who would be appointed to publicly funded posts in the cities of the eastern Mediterranean. Julian's own early education, on a remote imperial estate in Cappadocia, combined Christian teaching from Bishop George, whom he detested, and classical teaching from a court eunuch, Mardonius, whom he loved. As soon as it was safe to do so, he renounced the Christianity of his predecessor Constantius, son of Constantine. He called himself a 'Hellene' because he belonged to the ancient Greek culture whose authors expressed universal truth about divinity and humanity; and he called Christians 'Galilaeans', to emphasize the contrast with their reliance on the teaching of Jesus in Galilee, a remote part of an obscure province. He did not accept Christian claims to teach universal truth, both because they said that salvation came only through Jesus Christ, and because, in his experience, they did not live by their principles: too many of his family had been killed on the orders of a Christian emperor.

The cities of the eastern Mediterranean evidently realized that times had changed. Julian said that he would leave the choice of teachers to them, but, to show his concern for education, he

wanted the names of the teachers sent to him for approval. In a
follow-up letter, Julian explained that teachers must have high
moral standards, and his subjects need not be afraid to
acknowledge their religious beliefs, so Christians had a choice.
They could not with integrity teach children classical texts, such as
Homer, which in their view presented false beliefs about the gods.
So they must either teach Christian texts in church, or change
their beliefs and teach the classical texts which Julian believed to
be divinely inspired.

Governments in the ancient world did not take responsibility for
education, and Julian's letter applied only to posts which
depended on civic benefactors. But it was widely interpreted as an
attempt to ban Christians from all teaching, or even to exclude
Christian children from education, something that Julian
explicitly said he did not want to do. Even the consciously
impartial Ammianus, an admirer of Julian, disapproved of this
measure. Christian historians were much more outspoken about
the consequences of Julian's apostasy and of his plan to rebuild
the Jerusalem Temple, destroyed three centuries earlier by Roman
troops. From Julian's point of view, this plan had many
advantages. It was a challenge to Christians because Jesus had
said that the Temple would never be rebuilt; Julian could accept
Judaism as an ancient tradition which honoured its god by
sacrifice; and he wanted support from Jews in the Persian empire,
which he planned to invade. Christian authors wrote that the
rebuilding was halted first by an earthquake, then by fire blazing
from the foundations. Julian was killed, after a reign of eighteen
months, on a disastrous expedition into Persia. He had literally
burned his boats, so that his soldiers would know they could not
retreat; and Christian authors said that his dying words were 'you
win, Galilaean'.

A century and a half after Julian, in the time of Cassiodorus, came
an even more dramatic confrontation of classical and Christian
culture. Justinian, it is often said, closed Plato's Academy. It is a

good story: in the year 529 an intolerant Christian emperor ends the tradition of free intellectual enquiry which began 1,000 years earlier with Plato's Socrates, and which is fundamental for Western liberal values. The last head of the Academy leaves with his colleagues for the Persian court, because he cannot safely teach in the Roman empire. In the same year, Benedict founds his monastery at Monte Cassino. His enduring monastic rule establishes a way of life which depends on poverty, chastity, and obedience; or, from a different perspective, on rejection of society, of family, and of thinking for oneself.

'Justinian closed the Academy', like so many dramatic statements, needs to be qualified. It depends on the chronicle of John Malalas, a near contemporary who lived at Constantinople. The surviving summary of this chronicle includes a notice: 'the emperor sent a decree to Athens ordering that no one should teach philosophy or explain astronomy, nor should dice-casting happen in any city, because some dice-casters were found in Byzantium who were involved in terrible blasphemies'. This sounds like a familiar kind of ban on divination, which could take place by observation of the stars, as in astrology, or by apparently random events like dice-casting. But why, in this context, forbid the teaching of philosophy?

Some Platonist philosophers taught that the gods revealed their will in the workings of the universe. They included Damascius, then head of the Platonist school at Athens. Local Christians may have had some influence on Justinian's decree, or may have made sure that the governor of their region saw its relevance to Athens. In 1971, archaeologists found a house near the Areopagus where, early in the 6th century, images of pagan gods were defaced and a cross was inserted in a floor mosaic: this is evidence at least for strong feeling. Another law of Justinian reacted to the discovery that some Christians engaged in pagan practices. It required 'Hellenes', that is, pagans, to be instructed and baptized if they were not to lose their civil rights and property, and forbade them to teach or to receive a publicly funded salary, even when there was a previous imperial grant. The penalty for sacrifice and idol-worship was death. A further ban on bequests to pagans or pagan institutions meant that the Platonist school lost its funding. It could neither recruit students nor survive on its endowment, which was at risk of confiscation. Damascius was not noted for tact or ability to negotiate. In 531, he and six colleagues left for Persia; a year later they returned, protected by a new treaty with Persia, and we do not know what happened to them or to the teaching of Platonist philosophy at Athens. We do know that philosophers, Christian and non-Christian, continued to engage with the works of Plato.

Chapter 8
Decisive change?

To the east of the Nile and the Dead Sea were desert lands, home to nomad groups which were, as always, unpredictable and difficult to identify. The Semitic word 'Arab' referred both to the lands and to the nomadic peoples who lived there. Greek and Latin authors usually called these people Saraceni, and Ammianus offered a brief and sensational account of their customs, just as he did when discussing the Huns.

We have never wanted the Saracens as friends or as enemies. They ranged up and down the land, raiding whatever was to be found in a brief moment, like rapacious kites which see their prey from aloft and seize it with swift flight, or if they get nothing, do not stay around. The place of origin of these peoples extends from Assyria to the cataracts of the Nile. They are all warriors, half naked, wearing short dyed cloaks down to the groin, ranging widely on their swift horses and skinny camels in times of calm and of disturbance. None of them ever holds a plough or cultivates a tree or seeks a living by tilling the fields, but they always wander far and wide, without homes or fixed abodes or laws. They cannot bear to stay for long under the same sky, nor does the extent of one region ever satisfy them. Their life is a perpetual flight. Their wives are hired for a time by contract, and to give an appearance of marriage, the future spouse presents her husband with a spear and a tent as dowry; she will leave, if she chooses, after an agreed day. Both sexes yield to passion with unbelievable ardour. They wander so far in a lifetime that a woman marries in one place, gives birth in another, and raises her children far away; no scope for rest is allowed. They all eat the meat of wild animals, and there is abundance of milk to sustain them, and many kinds of plants, and any birds they can catch by fowling; I have seen many who are unaware of the use of corn and wine.

Christian writers used the name 'Saraceni' to find these peoples a history in Judaeo-Christian tradition. According to the book of Genesis, Sarah, wife of Abraham, was childless, and told Abraham to have a child for her with her Egyptian slave Hagar. God told Abraham that Hagar's son Ishmael would found a great nation, but that God's covenant would be with Sarah's son Isaac. When Isaac was born, many years after Ishmael, Abraham reluctantly sent Hagar and her son away to the desert. So the desert-dwelling Saraceni were, in a way, Sarah's people, and Christian writers also called them Hagarenes and Ishmaelites. In the early 5th century, the church historian Sozomen said that these other descendants of Abraham shared many customs with the Jews, including circumcision and abstinence from pork; some had forgotten their traditions and worshipped the gods of neighbouring peoples, some had returned to Jewish tradition, and some had converted to Christianity, inspired by the example of priests and monks who lived in the desert lands.

Ammianus said that the Romans did not want the Saracens as friends or as enemies, but by the 6th century the situation in the east was like that in the north. Roman and Persian rulers made alliances with leading families, and nomadic peoples settled, or made alliances with Roman or Persian commanders, or pushed into Roman or Persian territory. In the 7th century, there was a change. When Sophronius, patriarch of Jerusalem, preached his Christmas sermon in 634, he noted with regret that his people could not go out to Bethlehem to celebrate the birth of Jesus, because the Saraceni blocked the way. This had happened before,

15. Monastery of St Catherine, Sinai, fortified against Arab invasion

and Sophronius ascribed it to sin; he showed no awareness that this time was different, and the Arabs would not go back to the desert. Perhaps that same year, someone composed a dialogue, set in Carthage, between a Jew from Palestine who has been forced to convert to Christianity, and several other Jews whom he now wishes to convince. One of them brings news from his brother that a prophet has appeared among the Saracens, but not a true prophet, for he does not proclaim the Messiah, and he is armed with a sword.

After his Christmas sermon, Sophronius spoke more and more strongly of the danger, until in 637 he surrendered his city to the caliph Umar. The Saraceni were now part of a well-organized Arab army inspired by the new religious movement of Islam and its prophet Muhammad, who was born about the time the emperor Justinian died in 565, and himself died in 632. According to Islamic tradition, Sophronius invited Umar to pray in the

Church of the Holy Sepulchre, but Umar declined, fearing that his followers would take it over. Instead, he prayed among the ruins of the Temple Mount, and gave orders for a mosque to be built there. By the late 7th century, the Dome of the Rock faced the Church of the Holy Sepulchre, and Jerusalem was a holy city for all three religions which claimed descent from Abraham.

Defeat: Persians and Arabs

The Arab conquest was extraordinarily swift. It followed twenty years of devastating wars between the Roman empire, now centred on Constantinople, and the usual enemies: Persians in the east, barbarians in the Balkans. This time the barbarians were Avars, originally from Mongolia, and Slavs from the steppes. The Roman emperor Heraclius seized power in 610, after years of civil war which made the beginning of his reign disastrous. The Persians had invaded the Roman-controlled part of Armenia, and could now move their troops freely to attack anywhere from Armenia to Mesopotamia. Constantinople still controlled some of the territory reconquered by Justinian, but these regions around Ravenna and Carthage could not provide military or financial help. In 618, Heraclius had to end the distribution of free bread at Constantinople, because the local grain supply was not enough, and the imported supply from Africa and Egypt was not secure.

The Persians crossed the Euphrates to defeat Heraclius at Antioch. They took Syria; occupied Jerusalem and removed the relics of the cross of Christ to the Persian treasury; took Alexandria and claimed the Nile valley with its grain. In the north, they invaded Asia Minor and reached Chalcedon, across the Bosphorus from Constantinople; occupied Cyprus; and looted the mainland cities of Sardis, Ephesus, and Ancyra. Meanwhile, the Avars attacked in the Balkans, and Heraclius himself was almost captured. Constantinople was under threat from west and east, land and sea.

Somehow, Heraclius pulled an army together and fought back in Anatolia. He could tell his troops that this was a holy war, defending Christianity against the religion of the Persians; he ordered the destruction of a Zoroastrian fire-temple. Early Muslim authors, like Christians, praised him for defending the religion of Abraham against what they saw as Persian idolatry, until the time when he opposed Islam. In Constantinople, the patriarch Sergius organized resistance to the barbarians, and gave credit to the Virgin of Blachernae, whose icon was carried on the walls, for enabling them to withstand the Avar siege. The church at Blachernae, where the northern city wall met the Golden Horn, was completed by Pulcheria, sister of Theodosius II. She had also, it was said, imported from Palestine a robe believed to be the shroud of the Virgin, who left no bodily relics because she was taken up directly into heaven. In Thessalonica, further west, the patron saint Demetrios was credited with saving the town from the Slavs, who patrolled the Aegean Sea in their dug-out wooden boats.

Heraclius, who had suffered so much from the effects of civil war, was saved by civil war in Persia, which after 300 years brought the end of the Sassanian empire. He was able to demand the return of territory, and to restore the True Cross to Jerusalem. This was taken to be a sign of divine approval. But Heraclius had no more resources of manpower or finance, for the Persian invasions had seriously damaged the cities which provided his tax base. Moreover, the Christians in his territory were still divided by theology and tradition, and resented any attempt by an emperor to make them agree.

Six years after his great victory, the Arabs defeated Heraclius in Syria. Between 635 and 645, they took Damascus, Antioch, and Jerusalem, and defeated the Persian army; moved east from Syria, crossing the Euphrates to take Edessa and the Tigris to take the Persian capital Seleucia; and moved west to take Alexandria. From its capital at Damascus, the Umayyad dynasty

(661–750) ruled territory extending eastward to China and westward, through North Africa and Spain, to the Atlantic coast of southern France. In 674, Umayyad forces besieged Constantinople and blockaded the Bosphorus, but the city was protected by its walls, and the Byzantine fleet made effective use of 'Greek fire'. This was an incendiary weapon, recently developed or improved, which continued to burn in water; it was probably based on naphtha (crude oil) from the Black Sea. By the end of the 7th century, Arabic replaced Greek as the language of administration in the near east. Constantinople remained the capital of a Roman empire, fighting Slavs and Khazars and Bulgars to retain territory in Greece, the Balkans, and Asia Minor, resisting further Arab attacks, and negotiating or disputing with the pope and with other powers in western Europe.

The end of empire?

The coming of Islam used to provide a cut-off for the history of late antiquity. To historians who used mostly Greek and Latin sources, and who came from countries with a Christian rather than a Muslim tradition, it seemed obvious that the world had changed when the Mediterranean stopped being 'our sea', a Roman lake surrounded by Roman territory and ruled by Christian emperors. According to the 'Pirenne thesis', advanced by the Belgian historian Henri Pirenne in his *Mohammed and Charlemagne* (translated into English in 1939), the Roman empire in the west did not end when the last western emperor fell in 476. Rather, the break came in the 7th century when Islamic conquest of the Near East ended long-distance Mediterranean trade, and Charlemagne transformed the kingdom of the Franks into the Holy Roman Empire, which extended over much of western and central Europe. When Charlemagne was crowned emperor on Christmas Day 800, there were once again two Roman emperors, one in western Europe and one in Constantinople, but there was not a united Roman empire. Instead, there was Islamic rule over the east, south and west coasts of the Mediterranean, and divisions of power on the north coast. In the east, the Umayyad caliphate, based in Damascus and close to the Mediterranean, gave way in the mid-8th century to the Abbasid caliphate with its new capital at Baghdad; but there was still a strong Arab presence in the Mediterranean.

Historians and archaeologists continue to debate these changes. They ask whether Mediterranean-wide trade really declined, whether religious divisions really weakened resistance to the Arab invasions, and whether Arab conquest was really sudden and overwhelming, or whether, once again, it was more a question of accommodation and compromise. How dramatic and how permanent did the changes seem to the people who lived through them? One small example is a papyrus receipt written in Greek and Arabic, and precisely dated to 25 April 643. It records that Christophoros and Theodorakios, officials of Herakleopolis in Egypt, gave the emir Abdallah 65 sheep. The Greek version, written by the scribe and deacon Joannes, notes that the sheep were for the expenses of the Saracens. The Arabic version notes that some were butchered for the men on the ships, the cavalry and infantry. The names in this receipt illustrate a mixture of traditions. Herakleopolis was named after the Greek hero Herakles, son of Zeus and a mortal woman, famous for defeating monsters and for his amazing appetite for food, drink, and sex. Christophoros and Joannes have explicitly Christian names, and Theodorakios, 'a little present from God', is also Christian; Abdallah is 'servant of Allah'. The cover note records that this is a down-payment for 'the taxes of the first indiction', that is, in the payment cycle which continued from Roman rule, together with the bureaucracy which documented it.

Another example is the Mozarabic Chronicle of 754. 'Mozarabic', a word of Arabic origin, means 'Arabized', and refers to the Latin spoken by people who lived in Muslim-dominated areas of Spain. Arab armies crossed from Africa to Spain in 711, but the author of the chronicle does not suggest that this invasion is different in kind from the earlier Visigoth invasion. These glimpses suggest that the Arab takeover was not a traumatic and decisive change, but they may be misleading, because we have no full narrative. There are records of events in Greek and Syriac chronicles from the 7th and 8th centuries, and in the Armenian history ascribed to Sebeos. But there is no Greek history in the great classical tradition of interpreting war and politics, and the Arabic sources come from a later period and draw on a complex of legends. Scholars continue to debate the experience of the *dhimmi*, non-Muslims who were under the protection of Islamic rulers and paid a special tax, and to consider the changes to belief, practice, and culture which might result from conversion to Islam.

Interaction

The problem with a cut-off is that it cuts through continuing and interwoven strands. In the last half-century, those interconnections have become more evident to historians and their readers who live in multicultural societies. Arabic was the language of many Jews and Christians even before the Umayyad dynasty made it the language of administration. When Jewish, Christian, and Muslim theologians debated the relation of God to the world, they used the concepts of Greek philosophy, which was translated into Arabic, sometimes via Syriac. Christian texts were also translated into Arabic: the earliest known Bible texts are the Gospels, translated from Greek in the late 7th century. In the late 8th century, the Christian and Jewish scholars in Baghdad, the new capital of the Abbasid dynasty, included Timothy, patriarch of the Church of the East, who moved there from the Persian capital Ctesiphon. When the caliph asked him to translate the *Topica* of Aristotle, a work on dialectical reasoning, Timothy used a Syriac version, consulting the Greek text with the help of a Christian Arab who was secretary to a Muslim governor. He also wrote, in Syriac, an account of his discussion with the caliph on the merits of Christianity and Islam. This was translated into Arabic and was very popular among Christians. Timothy praised Muhammad for fighting idolatry, just as Abraham and Moses fought idolatry.

John of Damascus, in the early 8th century, is probably the earliest Christian writer to show some knowledge of Islam. He took John as his monastic name when he joined a community near Jerusalem, but his Arabic name was Mansur, and he is often depicted with a turban. John began his career in Damascus as a civil servant of the Umayyads. His family was Syrian, and his grandfather is said to have been an official at Damascus both before and after the Arab conquest. John seems never to have visited the lands which were still ruled from Constantinople, but his theology, written in Greek, had great influence there. From his perspective, Islam was one more heresy, the most recent of the 100 heresies he discussed, and like so many others, it was mistaken about the nature of Christ. John wrote briefly about Muhammad, the main beliefs of his followers and their objections to Christianity, and he knew a little about the Qur'an. Christians who differed from him on theology said that he was too close to Islam.

John contributed to the debate about icons, a longstanding question which became more prominent in the 8th century. It raises questions about cultural interaction and about demands for orthodoxy. The debate prompted the violent destruction called iconoclasm (literally, 'image-smashing'), and violent repression of disagreement. It may have been a response to Muslim theologians, who saw no need for intercessors between human beings and God, and challenged Christians to justify their veneration of icons and relics. Or debate may have intensified because icons did not always protect against Muslim invasions, and this strengthened the argument that veneration of icons in fact caused the invasions, as punishment for the sin of idolatry which is forbidden by the

Ten Commandments; just as in the Old Testament the people of Israel are punished by defeat and displacement when they turn from God to idols.

Greek has two words for 'image': *eidolon*, which means a shadow of the real thing, and *eikon*, 'likeness', which means a representation of the real thing. These words underlie 'idol' and 'icon'. Some philosophers argued that images of the gods must be misleading, because they were made by human hands and expressed only limited human understanding. Christians gladly borrowed their arguments to use against pagans: how can you worship a god when you know the man who made it? But other philosophers argued that the gods were willing to be present in such man-made images, and that traditional representations of gods were god-given and conveyed truth. Christian images raised theological questions which are central to Christian belief. We cannot see or paint God, but God became human in Christ: how is it possible to express or to represent this?

In late antiquity, some Christians believed, as some still believe, that there is a holy presence in an icon of Christ, or of Mary his mother, or of saints and angels. Perhaps it is easier to think of an icon as a window on the spiritual world, whereas a statue is more obviously a thing in the material world. In the mid-8th century, iconoclasts argued that icons made by a painter could not be holy in the same way that the Eucharist given by God, or a church consecrated to God, or the sign of the cross, were holy. Supporters of icons (called 'iconophiles', image-lovers) said that icons had a power which was not made by human hands: that was why the icon of the Virgin could repel Persian and Arab attacks on Constantinople. Some icons were said not to have been made by human hands at all, but to have come miraculously into existence. As so often, religious debate was entangled with politics and violence. Emperors summoned councils, produced official documents, and decreed that discussion must stop; bishops and monks were abused and exiled for holding the wrong view; there were stories of martyrs, and the end of iconoclasm was celebrated as the triumph of orthodoxy.

Closing down?

Late antiquity can be presented as a narrative of limitation and loss. The western Roman empire falls to Germanic peoples, the eastern Roman empire loses most of its territory to Arab invasions, the Mediterranean is no longer open for Roman trade. Even before these major losses, centralized bureaucracy takes resources and talent from flourishing classical cities. Society is frozen and hierarchical: people are legally bound to follow the family trade, or to stay on the land where they are in effect serfs, bound to the estate even though they are not slaves of the landholder. The classical city shrinks and declines as villages grow, and local magnates who live on their estates offer villagers the protection which city councillors and the empire can no longer give. Classical education disappears because governments have no use for the rhetorical skill it provided. Classical literary forms are no longer used, and after the reign of Heraclius, there is no history-writing in the great classical tradition. Classical texts are difficult to obtain, and classical learning is no longer a living culture; instead, it is the subject of handbooks and reference works like the *Etymologies* of Isidore, bishop of Seville. Works of classical philosophy are still read and translated, but they are not discussed in active philosophical schools.

It looks like a closing of the mind. Religious writers exhort men and women to give up their social and family ties for a life of self-deprivation and repentance, and biographers write in praise of their sufferings. Pagans, Jews, Manichaeans, heretics are not persecuted as brutally as Christians once were, but suffer legal constraint and casual violence, and Justinian denounces male homosexuality as an offence against nature which provokes the wrath of God. Intellectual energy is diverted into religious polemic, or collecting and copying the ideas of approved authorities, or classifying and denouncing heresies. Orthodoxy, 'right thinking', is required, especially in anyone who holds public office. In the 3rd century, the legal expert Ulpian said that nobody is punished for thinking, but from the 4th century onwards, Christian emperors responded to complaints against heretics:

> Arians, Macedonians, Pneumatomachi, Apollinarians, Novatiani or Sabbatiani, Eunomians, Tetraditae or Tesseracaedecatitae, Valentinians, Papianistae, Montanists or Priscillianists or Phrygians or Pepuzitae, Marcianists, Borboriani, Messalians, Eutychitae or Enthusiasts, Donatists, Audiani, Hydroparastatae, Tascodrogitae, Batrachitae, Hermeieciani, Photinians, Paulinians, Marcelliani, Ophites, Encratites, Apotactics, Saccophori, and those who have reached the lowest level of wickedness, Manichaeans, shall have no opportunity to meet and pray anywhere on Roman territory.

> We are informed that Manichaeans and Donatists, in particular, do not desist from their madness. [...] If anyone dares to involve himself with these forbidden and illicit things, let him not escape the noose of the innumerable previous decrees and of the law recently promulgated by Our Mildness, and let him not doubt that, if there have been any seditious gatherings, the darts of more intense concern have been roused and will be used.

The 'darts of more intense concern' included fines, confiscation of property, restrictions on giving or receiving inheritance, book-burning, and exile.

'Heresy' sums it up. The Greek word *'hairesis'* means 'choice'; by extension, it means a philosophical or medical school of thought. A philosopher could choose to follow the Stoics, or the Academics, or yet another interpretation of Platonism, or to reject them all in favour of Epicurus, who taught that the universe began in random collisions of atoms, there is no life after death, and the gods are unaffected by human concerns or by anything else. A doctor could choose to follow the Empiricists in using experience-based treatment with no general theory of disease, or the Methodists who thought that a diseased body is either too tight or too loose. Nothing worse would happen than counter-arguments from people who held different views, which might sometimes result in loss of business for doctors or loss of students for philosophers. But in a late antique Christian context, 'heresy' meant a dangerously wrong choice, a misguided belief which threatened orthodoxy and individual souls. So heretics were excommunicated, that is, excluded from communion with other members of a church. Sometimes their books were burned, and often their ideas survive only in so far as their opponents indignantly cite them and probably misrepresent them. Eusebius, writing his *History of the Church* at the time when Constantine came to power, presented orthodoxy as transmitted from the beginnings of Christianity through a succession of bishops, and triumphing over external persecution and over the far more dangerous internal threat of heresy, which results from the arrogance of heretics. Recent historians, especially those who serve on committees, have asked about the negotiations and the manipulations which determined what was orthodox.

But there are signs of hope. It was possible, though nerve-wracking, to negotiate with Attila the Hun. Barbarians could settle among Romans, intermarry with Romans, and form their own communities with kings and law codes. Christians and Jews and Muslims could discuss theology and philosophy and medicine. 'Heretical' interpretations survived in the range of late ancient Christianities. Perhaps historians have been too interested in cultural interchange among the elite, rather than in the impact of war and the loss of peace and prosperity; but they were right to emphasize the growing expectation that people should give in charity and rulers should show concern for the poor. Work on late antiquity has challenged sharp distinctions and clear-cut frontiers: Romans and barbarians, pagans and Christians and Jews and Muslims, orthodox and heretic believers, triumph and decline.

Some questions recur in the study of any period of history. What do you want to know about: great people and great events, individual lives, social and political systems, budgets, or beliefs? Who or what causes change: divine power or exceptional people, moral qualities or collective action, economic and environmental factors, or ordinary human muddle? What do we recognize in the past, is human nature a constant, and what matters most as our own world struggles with climate change, too little cash, and too many barbarians? Late antiquity offers some answers. We need some kind of empire, some accepted system of authority, to maintain order and allow interchange of goods and ideas. We also need the friars whom Gibbon heard singing amid the ruins of the Capitol, for charity and for challenge to accepted values. To return, finally, to Augustine: two cities are intermingled in this world. We do not know who belongs where, but we do know that citizenship depends on what we love.

Further reading

What and when is late antiquity? The time ranges of these volumes illustrate the different views of authors and their publishers:

Peter Brown, *The World of Late Antiquity: From Marcus Aurelius to Muhammad* (London, 1971 and many reprints) inspired a generation. Pictures and text combine to replace 'decline and fall' with cultural transformation. Marcus Aurelius was emperor in the mid-2nd century; Muhammad lived in the early 7th century. The publisher liked the alliteration, but the author takes the story further, to Harun al-Rashid in Baghdad in the late 8th century.

Peter Brown, *The Rise of Western Christendom*, 2nd edn. (Oxford, 2003) ranges even further, from 200 to 1000 and from Scandinavia to Mesopotamia, connecting the western European story with eastern Christianity. In his Introduction to the revised edition, Brown sets the context of debates on barbarians, the unity of Europe, and the continuity of Mediterranean trade in goods and ideas.

Averil Cameron, *The Later Roman Empire* (London, 1993) is a concise introduction to history and culture AD 284–430, that is, from Diocletian to (in practice) the division of the empire into Latin-speaking west and Greek-speaking east in the early 5th century. *The Mediterranean World in Late Antiquity* (London, 1993) covers the 5th and 6th centuries, specifically AD 395–600. *The Byzantines* (Oxford, 2010) offers reflection on 'Byzantium' and Byzantine society and an outline of Byzantine history from the foundation of Constantinople to its fall in 1453.

A. H. M. Jones, *The Later Roman Empire 284–602: A Social, Economic and Administrative Survey*, 2 vols (Oxford, 1964), affectionately known as the 'Jones Report on the State of the Roman Empire', is the place to look for information on how the system worked. It starts with Diocletian and ends with the death of the emperor Maurice, before the eastern empire lost territory to Persian and Arab invasions.

There is a recent return to traditional narrative history, with detailed discussion of war and politics, on the grounds that general theories about social or economic or intellectual causes cannot be tested except in narrative. Two good examples are Peter Heather, *The Fall of the Roman Empire: A New History* (London, 2005), mainly concerned with the west, and Stephen Mitchell, *A History of the Later Roman Empire AD 284–641* (Oxford, 2007), that is, from Diocletian to the death of Heraclius, which is especially helpful on the eastern empire.

Social history: Peter Garnsey and Caroline Humfress, *The Late Antique World*, 2nd edn. (Cambridge, 2009) covers the 3rd to the 5th centuries. It is especially strong on law and administration, and includes religion and morality, food supplies, and relief of poverty.

Reference works

Late Antiquity: A Guide to the Postclassical World, ed. Glen Bowersock, Peter Brown, and Oleg Grabar (Harvard, 1999) is a selective encyclopaedia, with longer and more thoughtful entries than encyclopaedias usually allow, for the period 250–800. The introductory essays are available separately as *Interpreting Late Antiquity: Essays on the Postclassical World* (2001).

Philip Rousseau (ed.), *A Companion to Late Antiquity* (Chichester, 2009) brings together essays by experts on the full range of late antiquity.

The *Cambridge Ancient History* provides authoritative overviews of political, military, cultural, and religious history. Three volumes of the revised edition are relevant to late antiquity: *The Crisis of Empire: AD 192–337* (vol. 12, 2005), edited by Alan Bowman, Peter Garnsey, and Averil Cameron; *The Late Empire: AD 337–425* (vol. 13, 1997), edited by Averil Cameron and Peter Garnsey; *Late Antiquity: Empire and Successors AD 425–600* (vol. 14, 2001), edited by Averil Cameron, Bryan Ward-Perkins, and Michael Whitby. There is some overlap with *The New Cambridge Medieval History*, vol. 1: *AD c. 500–c. 700*, edited by Paul Fouracre (2005).

The Oxford History of Byzantium, edited by Cyril Mango (2002),
   extends from the accession of Constantine in 306 to the fall of
   Constantinople in 1453.

The *Oxford Classical Dictionary*, 4th edn. (2010) includes many late
   antique entries. An *Oxford Dictionary of Late Antiquity*, edited by
   Oliver Nicholson, is in preparation.

Sources

Michael Maas, *Readings in Late Antiquity*, revised edn. (2009) offers
   a very wide range of material from the 3rd to the 8th centuries,
   including early Islamic sources and helpful maps.

A. D. Lee, *Pagans and Christians in Late Antiquity: A Sourcebook*
   (2000) offers good new translations, with explanations, of (mostly)
   4th-century material.

The series *Translated Texts for Historians 300–800* (Liverpool) offers
   annotated scholarly translations of texts in (so far) Greek, Latin,
   Syriac, Coptic, Old Irish, Armenian, Georgian, Arabic, ranging
   from chronicles and histories to records of church councils, letter
   collections, political treatises, and lives of saints.

Ammianus: selections translated by Walter Hamilton, *The
   Later Roman Empire (AD 354–378)* with notes by Andrew
   Wallace-Hadrill (Harmondsworth, 1986); see further John Matthews,
   The Roman Empire of Ammianus, revised edn. (Ann Arbor, 2007).

Procopius: *The Secret History*, translated by G. A. Williamson
   (Harmondsworth, 1966). See further Averil Cameron, *Procopius*
   (London, 1985).

Running the empire: Christopher Kelly, *Ruling the Later Roman Empire*
   (Cambridge, 2004) discusses the traditions of the late antique civil
   service, and suggests that the use of payments and connections was not
   'corruption', but a practical way of managing the imperial workload.

Jill Harries, *Law and Empire in Late Antiquity* (Oxford, 1999)
   explains how law worked and emphasizes the 'culture of criticism'
   which challenged late antique officials.

John Matthews, *Laying Down the Law* (Yale, 2000) studies the
   making of the Theodosian Code.

Military history

A. D. Lee, *War in Late Antiquity* (Blackwell, 2007) is a social history,
   exploring late antique attitudes to war, including Christian debate

on the uses of force; the economic impact of war and the cost of maintaining armies; and the social relationships of soldiers and their families.

The Cambridge History of Greek and Roman Warfare, vol. 2 (2008), edited by Philip Sabin, Hans Van Wees, and Michael Whitby, provides more traditional military history.

Some emperors

H. A. Drake, *Constantine and the Bishops* (Baltimore, 2000): Constantine and practical politics.

Shaun Tougher, *Julian the Apostate* (Edinburgh, 2007).

Michael Maas (ed.), *Cambridge Companion to the Age of Justinian* (Cambridge, 2005).

Some bishops

Augustine of Hippo has his own *Very Short Introduction*, by Henry Chadwick (Oxford, 2001, originally 1986). Peter Brown, *Augustine of Hippo*, revised edn. (London, 2000) is an outstanding account of Augustine in his social and intellectual context. Other important bishops: Philip Rousseau, *Basil of Caesarea* (Berkeley, CA, 1994); Neil McLynn, *Ambrose of Milan* (Berkeley, CA, 1994); and Dennis Trout, *Paulinus of Nola* (Berkeley, CA, 1999), all in the series *Transformations of the Classical Heritage*, edited by Peter Brown; J. N. D. Kelly, *Golden Mouth: The Story of John Chrysostom* (London, 1995).

Not a bishop: J. N. D. Kelly, *Jerome* (London, 1975); Stefan Rebenich, *Jerome* (London, 2002).

Barbarians, the Fall of Rome, and the 'Dark Ages'

Bryan Ward-Perkins, *The Fall of Rome and the End of Civilization* (Oxford, 2005) offers a lively argument for barbaric barbarians and sharp decline in the quality of life, especially in the western empire.

Christopher Kelly, *Attila the Hun: Barbarian Terror and the Fall of the Roman Empire* (London, 2009) presents 'Attila the Gangster'.

Wolf Liebeschuetz, *The Decline and Fall of the Roman City* (Oxford, 2001) considers textual and material evidence from the west and the east.

Andy Merrills and Richard Miles, *The Vandals* (Chichester, 2010) brings together texts, archaeology, and interpretations of Vandals as destroyers and as noble barbarians.

James J. O'Donnell, *The Ruin of the Roman Empire* (New York, 2008) is especially interesting on Theoderic, Cassiodorus, and Justinian.

Gothic Bible: http://www.wulfila.be accessed 15 September 2010.

Post-Roman Europe and challenges to the 'Dark Ages': Julia Smith, *Europe after Rome: A New Cultural History 500–1000* (Oxford, 2005); Chris Wickham, *Framing the Early Middle Ages: Europe and the Mediterranean 400–800* (Oxford, 2005).

Religion

Peter Brown, *The Body and Society* (New York, 1988) argued that asceticism allowed men and women to reclaim their lives from the relentless purposes of society. The introduction to the revised edition (New York, 2008) sets this argument in the context of debates on the body.

Gillian Clark, *Christianity and Roman Society* (Cambridge, 2004) is a relatively short introduction to a very large subject.

Sidney H. Griffith, *The Church in the Shadow of the Mosque: Christians and Muslims in the World of Islam* (Princeton, NJ, 2008).

Robert Hoyland, *Seeing Islam as Others Saw It: A Survey and Evaluation of Christian, Jewish and Zoroastrian Writings on Early Islam* (Princeton, NJ, 1997).

Robert Markus, *The End of Ancient Christianity* (Cambridge, 1990) prompted much debate on Christian and secular identity.

Stephen Mitchell and Peter Van Nuffelen (eds.), *One God* (Cambridge, 2010) is a collection of essays on 'pagan monotheism'.

Tessa Rajak, *The Jewish Dialogue with Greece and Rome* (Boston, MA, 2002) collects her papers on religious and cultural interaction.

Seth Schwartz, *Imperialism and Jewish Society, 200 BCE to 640 CE* (Princeton, NJ, 2004).

Richard Valantasis (ed.), *Religions of Late Antiquity in Practise* (Princeton, NJ, 2000) is a collection of texts from all the main religious movements, including Manichaeism and philosophical monotheism.

Literature and visual art: Michael Roberts, *The Jeweled Style: Poetry and Poetics in Late Antiquity* (Cornell, 1989); Jas Elsner, *Imperial Rome and Christian Triumph* (Oxford, 1998); on icons, see Robin Cormack, *Writing in Gold* (London, 1985).

Chronology

Early 390s	Ammianus completes his history (AD 96–378; only 354–78 extant)
395	Augustine becomes bishop of Hippo Regius. Theodosius I dies; Stilicho regent; empire divided into Greek-speaking east and Latin-speaking west
Late 4th century	Bishops: Basil of Caesarea, Gregory of Nazianzus, Gregory of Nyssa, John Chrysostom; Ambrose of Milan, Paulinus of Nola
	Jerome (not a bishop) biblical scholar
	Orators: Libanius (314–93), Themistius
410	Goths under Alaric sack Rome
413–28	Augustine writes *City of God*
415	Hypatia murdered
417	Orosius finishes his 'History Against the Pagans'
430	Augustine dies
431	Vandals take Carthage
437	Theodosian Code completed
448	Embassy of Priscus to Attila the Hun (reigned c. 439–53)
450	Council of Chalcedon rejects 'monophysite' theology
455	Vandals sack Rome
459	Simeon Stylites dies
476	Deposition of Romulus Augustulus, traditionally the last western emperor
493–526	Theoderic the Ostrogoth rules from Ravenna
c. 525	Boethius executed
526–34	Amalasuntha, regent of the Ostrogothic kingdom
535–6	Theodahad rules the Ostrogoths
527–65	Justinian emperor
528	*Corpus Iuris Civilis* completed
532	Nika riot
542	Plague reaches Constantinople
550	Procopius publishes *History of the Wars*
c. 554	Cassiodorus returns to the Vivarian
c. 565–632	Muhammad
619–41	Heraclius emperor
637	Arab conquest of Jerusalem
651	Sassanian dynasty ends in Persia
661–750	Umayyad caliphate at Damascus
from 750	Abbasid caliphate at Baghdad
c. 750	John of Damascus dies
800	Coronation of Charlemagne

Index

Late Antiquity

Expand your collection of
VERY SHORT INTRODUCTIONS

READING GUIDES

Very Short Introductions

Whether you are part of a reading group wanting to discuss non-fiction books or you are eager to further your thinking on a *Very Short Introduction*, these reading guides, written by our expert authors, will provoke discussions and help you to question again, why you think what you think.

ANCIENT WARFARE
A Very Short Introduction
Harry Sidebottom

Greek and Roman warfare differed from other cultures and was unlike any other forms of warfare before and after. The key difference is often held to be that the Greeks and Romans practised a 'Western Way of War'. All aspects of ancient warfare are thoroughly examined – from philosophy and strategy to the technical skills needed to fight. He also explores the ways in which ancient society thought about conflict.

Taking fascinating examples from the Iliad, Tacitus, and the Persian Wars, Sidebottom uses arresting anecdotes and striking visual images to show that the understanding of ancient war is an ongoing process of interpretation.

> 'This is a little book which is jam-packed with ideas and insights. This book offers an interesting and invigorating read.'
>
> **TLS**

> 'I am addicted to this series of pocket-portable introductory lectures – they provoke active and reactive thought.'
>
> **The Guardian**

www.oup.com/vsi